A GLOSSARY

OF

COLONIAL ARCHITECTURAL

TERMS

By

NORMAN MORRISON ISHAM

with

A BIBLIOGRAPHY OF BOOKS
1880–1930

The Dating of Old Houses.

BY HENRY C. MERCER, SC.D., DOYLESTOWN, PA.

American Life Foundation & Study Institute
Watkins Glen, New York
1976

© 1968 American Life Foundation & Study Institute
Watkins Glen, New York 14891
A Glossary of Colonial Architectural Terms
by Norman Morrison Isham
was originally published by The Walpole Society © 1939
Library of Congress Catalogue Card Number: 68-20804

SECOND PRINTING 1976

ISBN: 0-89257-009-1

A GLOSSARY

OF

COLONIAL ARCHITECTURAL

TERMS

ABACUS. The crowning mem-

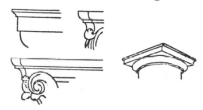

ber of a capital, q. v. It varies with the order used.

ANCHOR. A bar of wrought iron fastened to the end of a beam and built into a brick or stone wall, or sometimes carried through the wall and secured by a cross-iron in the shape of an S.

ARCH. An arrangement of radiating wedge-shaped stones or of

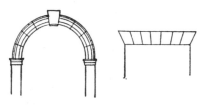

brick with wedge-shaped joints which are set in the form of a curve, a half-circle, a segment or an ellipse, or even on a level line. The stones or bricks are called voussoirs, q. v. The word is used for the same forms when built up of wood.

ARCH ORDER. An arch which has on the pier at either side an engaged column or a pilaster, q. v.,

carrying an entablature with or without a pediment. It is rare, but an analogous form is very common in wooden door frames in later work.

ARCHITRAVE. The lowest

ARCHITRAVE. (Cont'd) member of an entablature, *q. v.*, resting on the abaci of the column

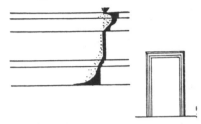

capitals. Also used of both the horizontal and the vertical stone or wood trimming or casing around a square or rectangular opening.

ARCHIVOLT. The moulding of an architrave carried around the face of an arch, *q. v.*

ASHLAR. Stone cut square so that the exposed faces are rectangles. *See* Rustication.

ASTRAGAL. A small half round moulding. It generally has a fillet on one or both sides. *See* Bead, Neck Moulding.

ATTIC. A modern word for the garret.

BACK BAND. The outer moulding of a door or window casing, *q. v.*

BALUSTER. A turned or rectangular upright supporting a stair rail. It is set between this rail and the stair step, or the floor, or the top of a closed string. *See* Stair. Used also on the outside of a building.

BALUSTRADE. The combi-nation of posts, rail and balusters of a stair, *q. v.*, or of posts, bottom rail, top rail and balusters above a cornice on the outside of a building.

BAR. A small moulded piece of wood separating the panes of glass in a sash. It suc-ceeded the lead calme or came, *q. v.*

BARGE BOARD. A false raft-er set a little out from the clap-boards of a gable. It protected the ends of the clapboards and con-cealed the underside of the roof board.

BASE. The moulded block of stone or wood on which a column, pilaster or pier directly rests. It stands upon a square block, the plinth. The mouldings vary with the order used. *See* Order.

BASE BOARD. A board of more or less width at the bottom of a wooden outside wall, or of a plastered inside wall.

BASE COURSE. An elabo-rately moulded base board or a stone course, plain or moulded, above the brick or stone under-pinning. Moulded brick is often used.

BAT. A portion of a brick bro-ken off and used to fill spaces. *See* Closer.

BATTEN. A board, narrow or wide, nailed on the back of two or more other boards to hold them together as in a door made of sheathing.

BATTEN DOOR. A door made in the manner described.

BEAD. A half round moulding, the same as an astragal, *q. v.*

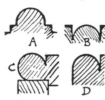

——QUIRKED. A bead at the corner of a board or of two boards. It has a quirk or sinkage on one or both sides.

——SUNK. A bead which does not project. It is necessarily quirked on both sides.

BEARER. A rather narrow beam fixed to the studs on the inside of an outer wall, to carry the ends of the second story floor joists; the device is still in use as a "ribbon" about 1⅛" by 5" or 6".

BEATER. A stick used in England and perhaps here also in early times, to "beat" mortar and thus mix the lime and sand. *See* Wren Society, volume x.

BED MOULD. A moulding beneath the soffit or "planceer," or beneath the modillion band or the dentil band, *q. v.*, of a cornice. *See* Order.

BEDROOM. This generally refers to a sleeping room on the ground floor of the house. *See* Chamber.

BELT COURSE. A course of stone, flush with the wall or projecting, or several projecting courses of brick, or a flush or projecting course of wood. Used on the outside of a building to mark the floor line or to bring about an apparent reduction in height.

BOLECTION MOULDING. A heavy moulding partly on the panel and partly on the stile or

rail of the panelwork. It was constantly used in England by Wren and is generally called, in the accounts "bolection work." It was used a good deal here before the Revolution. The derivation of the word is not known. It may possibly come from the Dutch *beleggen* akin to Ger. *belegen*, to trim or edge. Belection and balection occur, as well as bilection which appears in "a bilection plane" in a Providence inventory of 1787.

BOND. The alternation of the vertical joints in the courses of a brick or stone wall, so that these joints do not come over each other; and the laying of the bricks or stones, some across and some

BOND. (Cont'd)
lengthwise of the wall. *See* Closer.

——ENGLISH. In this form of bond, one or more courses of stretchers, or bricks laid lengthwise, are used to one course of headers, or bricks laid crosswise. *See* Closer. In later work

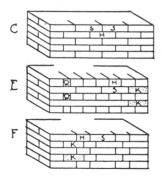

the ratio varies from one to three up to one to seven and even one to eleven. This last arrangement is hardly to be called English Bond. E.

——GARDEN WALL. An English name for three courses of stretchers to one of headers in brick work.

——FLEMISH. In this the headers and stretchers alternate in each course with the center of each header over the center of the stretcher below. F.

——COMMON. All the stones or bricks are stretchers. Used in stonework. In brick it is quite late. C.

——ALL HEADERS. Occasional in Maryland. It may have come from Western France.

BRACE. A stick set at forty-five degrees between two beams

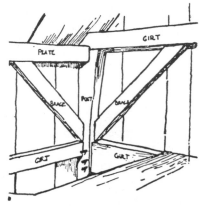

which meet at right angles. This framing forms a triangle which will not change its shape as long as the joints hold.

——BOARDING. Outer boarding put on diagonally at the feet or tops of posts.

BRACKET. A curved or angular projection at the top of a post to enable it to support two or three beams. *See* Post Bracket, Post Flare. The scroll on the end of a step in an open-string stair.

BUTTERY. Originally bottlery (Fr. *bouteillerie*), the place where the beer and ale were distributed. Later it came to mean the same as pantry, *q. v.*

CABLE. A bead set in the low-

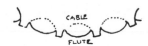

er third of the flute, *q. v.*, of a column or pilaster.

CAMBER. The thickening or raising of a beam in the center which is thus made higher than the ends.

CAME (*calme, calamus,* a reed). The H-shaped lead strip

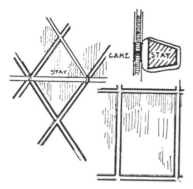

which holds the window glass. *See* Quarrel. It was made in a miniature rolling mill.

CAPITAL. The crowning member of a column or pilaster. Two forms, the Tuscan and Doric, have mouldings only, which in the Doric may be carved. The Ionic is distinguished by its volutes, of the Classic or flat type, or the angular Scamozzi form which is almost exclusively used. The Corinthian and Composite are floriated and the latter has angular volutes. The Tuscan and Composite are practically never used. *See* Order.

CARPENTER. Originally in England the workman who did the heavy framing. *See* Joiner.

CARRIAGE. The wood framing supporting the finished string and steps of a stair. *See* Stayer.

CARTOUCH. A sort of shield with scroll-work border.

CASEMENT. A frame of wood or iron filled with glass set in cames or bars and hung between mullions, to which it is hinged to swing outward. It was sometimes merely the leaded glass alone, fastened in place but not hung. Also the vertical half of a window glazing with no mullions. This swings outward on hinges and is fastened where the two halves meet in mid-opening.

CASING. The mouldings or flat strip around a door or window on the inside. *See* Architrave. In old wood-plastered partitions the frame and architrave are the same with a slight moulding.

CAVETTO (OR COVE). A hollow moulding about a quarter circle or quarter ellipse in profile. *See* Moulding.

CEILING. The underside of the floor above a room, or of a roof. An old name for sheathing, or panelling, *q. v.*

CEILING JOIST. Generally the same as collar beam, *q. v.*, but in England, and here in very rare cases, joists for the ceiling are found which are independent of the floor joists of the floor above.

CHAIR RAIL. A moulding—really a surbase, *q. v.*—carried around a room which has no panelling.

CHAMBER. A sleeping room in the second story. Probably also used for the whole second floor, as in the old expression "Up Chamber" — pronounced somewhere between chahmber and chammber—for the second story of a house.

CHAMFER. Strictly, and in its simplest form, a bevel along the edge of a beam to take off the sharp corner; (*a*) in more elabo-

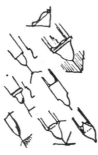

rate work it became moulded with a fillet at each corner and a quarter-round (*b*), or an ogee (*c*), between them. These ogee chamfers are sometimes four inches wide (*d*).

CHAMFER-STOP. A way of bringing the chamfer to an end before the post meets a beam or a beam meets another beam. These stops vary through the forms shown.

CHIMNEY. (Lat. *caminus*, a forge.) A fireplace and its flue. The stack above the roof of the house.

——PIECE. A wood or stone frame for a fireplace. *See* Stack. Those of wood were often carried to the ceiling.

CHYMOL. *See* Jimmer.

CLAPBOARD. A thin board a little over four feet in length riven radially, or with the grain from a "bolt", a little over four feet in length cut from a tree trunk. In early work of oak; later of pine. The word, in England about 1700, meant an unwrought barrel stave. *See* Weather Boarding.

CLOSER. Part of a brick inserted to make the joints in the alternate courses of either English or Flemish bond come over each other. A quarter of a brick, or quarter "bat" next to the first stretcher is called a queen closer. A three-quarter "bat" at the last stretcher is a king closer. *See* Bond, E, *q* and *k*.

CLOSED STRING. An outer string of a stair in which ends of the steps do not show, but which has a straight pitch from post to post. *See* String.

COIN. *See* Quoin.

COLLAR BEAM (OR COLLAR JOIST). A tie between two rafters about six feet above the garret floor. It really acts in many cases more as a brace than as a tie.

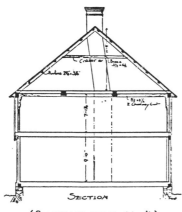

SECTION

(See COLLAR BEAM *opposite)*

COMMON RAFTER. A rafter reaching from the plate, *q. v.*, to the peak of the roof and supported in the middle by a purlin, *q. v. See* Truss.

CONSOLE. A scroll-shaped bracket supporting a shelf or a cornice.

COPING. The covering of a wall which carries no roof. It may be of stone, brick, or wood.

CORBEL-STEPS (Eng.), CORBIESTEPS (Scot.). The square offsets in a Dutch gable, New Amsterdam.

CORNICE. The crowning member of an entablature. It varies with the order used. Also the mouldings at the edge of the roof. These generally follow the orders. *See* also Eaves. The mouldings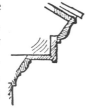

of wood or plaster at the angle of wall and ceiling in a room.

COUPLES. An old word for pairs of rafters.

CROSS-GARNET. *See* Hinge.

CROSSETTE. A double mitering of the architrave at the upper corner of a door or window, or other opening.

CURB PLATE. The plate under the change of pitch in a gambrel roof.

——ROOF. *See* Gambrel.

CURTAIL STEP. The bottom step of a stair the rail of which ends in a scroll, *q. v.*, which the edge of the step follows.

CYLINDER. A modern word for the curved part of the front-string of a circular stair or a straight stair with a circular half turn. The old newel, *q. v. See* also Stair.

DADO. The plain space in a pedestal between the base and the surbase (*q. v.*). The same space in panelling. Wrongly applied to a surbase or to a chair rail, *q. v. See* Pedestal.

DENTILS. Small blocks in a classic cornice. *See* Order, Corinthian.

——BAND. A band not cut into separate dentils or, in woodwork, the band to which the dentils are nailed.

DENTICULAR. A Doric cornice which has dentils and no mutules. Seldom used unless for inside work. Neither Batty Langley, 1741, nor Paine, 1794, show it.

DOG-LEGGED STAIR. One type of solid-newel stair, *q. v.*

DOME. A roof of wood or a ceiling of plaster generally in the form of a half or a smaller segment of a sphere. Sometimes octagonal in plan with a pointed section.

DORMER. A vertical window in the slope of a roof. *See* Lutheran. Luthern occurs as late as 1827 in Worcester's American edition of Walker's Johnson.

DORMANT TREE. An old name for a summer, *q. v.*

DOVETAIL. The end of a beam cut into a truncated wedge to prevent it from pulling out of the framing.

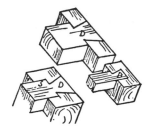

——HALF. One side of a beam cut as a wedge while the other is straight.

——SHOULDERED. Where part of the dovetailed beam is let into its supporter.

DOWEL. A piece of hard wood used to hold two boards together.

DRAGON BEAM. A diagonal summer pojecting over an outer

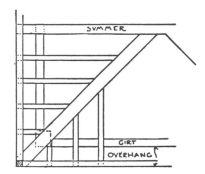

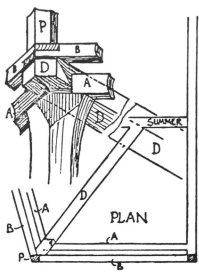

corner of a house to carry an overhang.

DRAW-BORE TENON. A tenon in which the pinhole does not align with that in the cheeks or sides of the mortise, but is kept nearer the inside of the mortised beam so that when the pin is driven it has to drag the shoulders of the tenon close against the mortised beam or post. This is apt to cause difficulty in the proper taking down of old work which is to be set up again, as the oak pins may be found so bent that they cannot be "drifted," or driven out.

DRIPSTONE. A ledge in a chimney just above the slope of the roof and sometimes also just above the ridge, to prevent water from following the face of the masonry into the house.

EASE. A curve in a handrail connecting a descending rail to the post cap at its foot.

EAVES. The projection of rafters, boarding and shingles beyond the face of the wall below. The early form of watershed which preceded the

classic form of cornice with its mouldings.

EGG AND DART. Also called Egg and Tongue. An ornament

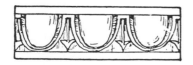

applied to the ovolo or quarter-round moulding, *q. v.*

ENGLISH BOND. A course of headers alternating with a course of stretchers. *See* Bond, English; Closer.

ENTABLATURE. The whole weight or superstructure carried

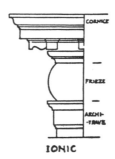

IONIC

by the columns or pilasters of an order. It consists of architrave, frieze, and cornice, *q. v.*

ENTASIS. The curve of the line in which a column diminishes in diameter as it rises.

ENTRY. The space into which outside door of a house opened. It might be a space in front of the stairs and chimney, or it might be what is now called a hall running from front to back of the house. It is a remnant of the "screens" of an old English house.

EXTRADOS. The line of the backs of the voussoirs of an arch. *See* Arch, Intrados, Voussoir.

FASCIA. A flat band. One of the divisions of an Ionic or Corinthian architrave, *q. v.*

FEATHEREDGED. Brought to a sharp edge, triangular in sec-

FEATHEREDGED. (Cont'd) tion, as in one side of a clapboard or in the sides of a panel or one or more sides of a sheathing board. *See* Bolection Moulding, Panel.

FESTOONS. Drapery or flowers carved as drooping on the

place to keep the brick or stone from burning out.

FIREPLACE. The space in the chimney stack where the actual fire is built. It consists of the floor which has the hearth in front and the underfire behind, the jambs at

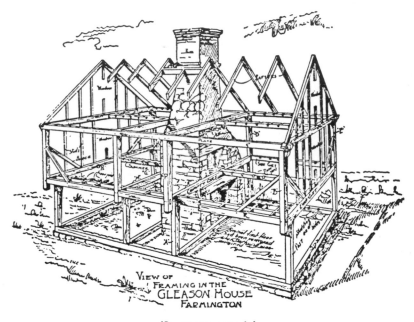

VIEW OF
FRAMING IN THE
GLEASON HOUSE
FARMINGTON

(*See* FRAME *opposite*)

walls as if hung at intervals from ornamental supports.

FILLET. A small square member between two mouldings or between a moulding and a wider flat surface. A small projecting strip. One of the narrow vertical divisions separating the flutes of a column or pilaster.

FIREBACK. A cast-iron plate set up against the back of a fire-

the sides, which are sometimes set at right angles to the back, with a square corner or a quadrant, but most often set on a bevel.

——COUNT RUMFORD. Triangular in plan. *See* Rumford.

FLARE. A modern word to describe a post which, instead of having a bracket, *q. v.*, at its top increases in size throughout its whole height. *See* Post Flare.

FLEMISH BOND. Headers and stretchers alternating in the same course. *See* Bond, F, Closer.

FLUSH. Surfaces which, whether continuous or not, are in the same plane.

FLUTE. A vertical hollow, in a series decorating the surface of a column or pilaster.

FLYERS. Steps set at right angles to the axis of a stair, in distinction from winders, *q. v. See* Stair.

FOOTPACE. A considerable space set lengthwise in a straight flight of stairs, as a resting place. *See* Stair, Half-Pace, H, and Quarter Pace, Q.

FRAME. The assemblage of light and heavy timbers which carried the covering and filling of sides, floors and roof. *See also* Summer. The head jambs and sill, *q. v.*, put together, to form a door or window opening.

(See illustration opposite)

FRET. A pattern jig-sawed out of thin wood and applied to a surface.

FRIEZE. The second or middle member, in height, of an entablature. It rests on the architrave and carries the cornice.

——CUSHION. A convex face given to the frieze by Palladio and handed on by Batty Langley and William Pain. *See* Order, Ionic.

FROW, FROE. A tool with the blade set at right angles to the handle. Its edge was on the bottom of the blade, the back of

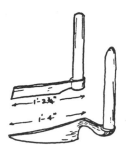

which was struck with a mallet or a maul. It was used by coopers to rive barrel staves and by carpenters in getting out the old riven laths and clapboards.

FURRING. Bringing the faces of joists or studs into line with each other by nailing on thin strips of wood.

GABLE. The outline of the wall at the end of a roof from the eaves or cornice to the peak or ridge.

GAIN. A space cut out of a post to relieve the tenon of a girt, or cut from a girt to receive the end of a stud.

GALLETING. Inserting small stones, black or dark blue, in the wide mortar joints of a stone underpinning.

GAMBREL. A form of roof in two slopes on each side, the lower slopes steep like an early roof, the upper rather flat. Probably de-

GAMBREL. (Cont'd)
rived from the French Mansard, so called, and used for the same

purpose, to prevent an enormous height of the steep roof in the wide houses of the later type.

GARRET. The story under the roof and above the second story. In a story-and-a-half house it would still be called the chamber.

GAUGED. Used to describe brick cut to fit in an arch ring, or shaped to a pattern by cutting instead of by moulding. It is also used of the plaster of Paris added to lime for finishing plaster, and to lime building mortar also, formerly, to make it set more rapidly.

GEMMELS. *See* Chymol, Jimmer, Hinge.

GIMMER. *See* Jimmer.

GIRT. A beam in the outer wall of a building to receive the ends of the floor joists. It carries the summer when the latter does not rest on a post. *See* Frame, Summer.

GOOSENECK. A workman's term for a ramp, *q. v.*

GORGE. A hollow moulding, the same as the cove or cavetto, *q. v.*

GROUNDSILL (GRUNDSILL, GRUNSEL). An old name for the sill, *q. v.*, also Frame.

GUTTER. A 6 x 10 or thereabouts, hollowed out is sometimes found as a part of the main cornice, where it serves as does the familiar wooden dug-out gutter.

HALF-PACE. The landing in a double-run stair where a half turn is made. *See* Quarter-Pace, Footpace.

HALF-ROUND. The Torus moulding. *See* Moulding.

HALL. The living room and kitchen of a one-room seventeenth-century house. When the kitchen was moved into a lean-to or was in the cellar, it retained its name. It was the descendant of the old English hall and was never a passageway. Sometimes called fire room in one-room houses.

HALL CHAMBER. The room above the hall.

HAND RAIL. The rail of a stair.

HEAD. The lintel or top-piece of a door or window frame. *See* Jamb.

HEADERS. Bricks laid across the wall so that their ends show. *See* Bond.

HEADING COURSE. A course all headers.

HERRINGBONE WORK.

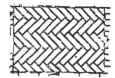

Bricks laid at an angle of forty-five degrees.

HINGE. The mechanism for hanging doors to swing.

——LOOP. Two bent pieces of metal looped together. Mostly

used in old chests, they sometimes have survived in houses.

——SNIBELL. This is the true hinge. A long bar sometimes with a well-wrought outer end

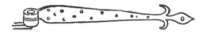

and an inner end formed as an eye which went over a snibell (possibly snipe bill), a word now superseded by "pintle."

——JIMMER. From old Fr. *jumel* (*jumeau*) a twin. An inseparable hinge. The snibell form could be taken apart, since the door could be lifted off. With the jimmer the hinge must be taken from the frame to release the door.

——VARIANTS OF THE JIMMER.

Cock's Head.

Cross Garnet. T-shaped

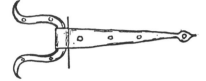

with the head on the jamb. Sometimes quite ornate.

H hinge.

HL hinge. Pew door H.

HIP (OR HIPPED) ROOF. A roof which pitches from all four walls of the building it covers.

HIP. An external angle formed by the meeting of two roof sur-

faces of a hip roof. The opposite of a valley, *q. v.*

HIP-GAMBREL. A combination of a gambrel and a hip roof

HIP-GAMBREL. (Cont'd)
with the two small gables of the gambrel. Very common in Newport. It seems rare elsewhere.

IMPOST. A horizontal block, plain or moulded, from which an arch springs.

INTRADOS. The under side of the ring of voussoirs forming an arch. *See* Voussoir, Extrados.

ITALIAN MOULDING. The wide heavy moulding surrounding a fireplace opening in early panel-

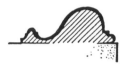

ing. So called in Wren's time. It came to us from England which it reached from Italy through France.

JAMB. The side of a window or door frame, of an opening in a wall, or of a fireplace.

JERKIN-HEAD. The truncation, or bevelling off, of a gable.

JET. A carpenter's word for a cornice. An overhang.

JETTY. An overhang, *q. v.*

JIMMER. Literally a twin, Old Fr. *jumel* (*jumeau*). A hinge the parts of which are not separable. *See* Hinge, Chymol, Gemmel, Gimmer.

JOINER. A carpenter who did inside finish and panelling. A cabinet maker. Older signs used to read "Carpenter and Joiner." *See* Carpenter.

JOINTER. A long plane for truing up the edges of boards.

JOISTS. The smaller beams which directly supported the floor between the girts and the summer. Later they spanned the whole room from girt to girt. *See* Frame, Summer.

KEYSTONE. A voussoir in the center of the arch ring, made longer than the others. It is often carved, sometimes has side pieces, and is sometimes shaped with side scrolls. It is so called because it is set last and closes the arch. *See* Arch.

KING POST. A post which originally in mediaeval work stood on a heavy beam and actually supported the upper ends of the rafters. It has long been really a tie which hangs from the peak of the roof and supports the tie beam. *See* Truss, Queen Post.

KNEE. A bracket, generally rectangular, made out of a naturally bent limb of a tree. Generally used to tie a corner horizontally. *See* Rafter, Knee.

LANTERN. A structure square, octagonal or round in plan, sometimes of considerable height, set on a roof generally as an observation point, but often for mere appearance, or on a dome to give light. The sides may be open or glazed at pleasure.

A short stage in a steeple consisting of the belfry as at Christ Church, Cambridge; or of the belfry with a short stage above it.

LATCH. A contrivance of wood or metal for keeping a door closed. It consists of a bar and a keeper; with a means of raising the bar and a means of pulling the door open or shut.

LATCHSTRING. A piece of raw hide fastened to the bar of a wooden latch and carried through the door so as to hang free on the outside. By pulling it down the bar could be raised, but with the string on the inside the door could not be opened.

LEAN-TO. A room or line of rooms with a roof which seems to

lean against a larger mass. A house with such a roof at its back.

LIGHTS. The panes of glass in a window as an eight-"light", or twelve-"light" window. In early times the open spaces between the mullions, q. v., of a two-, three-, or four-"light" window.

LINTEL. A heavy beam of stone or wood over an opening.

LOCK, BOX. An iron mechanism encased in a wood or iron case which was fastened to a rail of the door.

LOCK RAIL. A horizontal strip or rail between the panels of a door above mid-height. It was of considerable width to receive on its face the usual box lock which was applied to it.

LUTHERAN WINDOW. Luthorn, Luthern (Fr. *lucarne*). A dormer window, *q. v.*

MANTEL. Originally a wood-and-plaster or a stone hood, later a vertical wall over the fireplace. The eighteenth-century English word for what we know as a mantel is chimney piece, *q. v. See also* Italian moulding.

MANTLETREE. A heavy oak beam over the fireplace opening to carry the masonry above. It is always chamfered in early work and sometimes moulded.

METOPE. The space between two triglyphs in the frieze of the Doric order. *See* Order, Doric; and Triglyph.

MODILLION. A form of bracket in the cornice of the Corinthian and Composite orders, and of Palladio's and Scamozzi's Ionic.

MORTISE. A rectangular sinkage in a beam to receive a tenon,

MORTISE. (Cont'd)

q. v., cut on the end of another beam. The pin or treenail driven through both beams ties them together.

MOULDING. An ornamental shaping of the internal or external angles or surfaces or of the faces of a beam board, or other solid, or of a group of these, into forms copied from those used in stone-

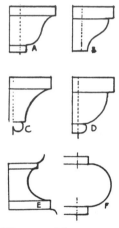

work. The usual forms are shown in the illustration: (*a*) Cyma Recta, Cyma, or Crownmould; (*b*) Cyma Reversa or Ogee; (*c*) Cavetto or Cove; (*d*) Ovolo or Quarter Round; (*e*) Scotia or Hollow; (*f*) Torus or half round. *See also* Astragal, Bead.

MULLION. An upright piece of wood, generally moulded in early work, and rebated and beaded later, which divided the lights, *q. v.*, of a casement window. *See* Window, Mullioned.

MUNTIN. The strip of wood separating the panes of a sash or casement. The same as a bar, *q. v.*

MUTULE. A sort of flat bracket in the mutular Doric Order. *See* Order, Doric.

NEWEL. To-day, in this country this means the lowest post of the stair, that at the start. The others are called intermediates. Anciently it meant the post around which a circular stair wound in its ascent. Later the word came to mean the opening or open space around which the stair rose, whether this space was square, circular, or elliptical. This was called an open newel while the post around which the corkscrew stair rose was called a closed newel. The colonial planners generally employed the open newel. It seems impossible now to tell when the modern meaning, that of the lowest post, came into use. *See* Stair.

NOSING. The rounded projection of the tread of a step beyond the face of the riser or of the string.

OGEE. The cyma reversa moulding, convex above and concave below. *See* Moulding.

ORDER. The definite arrangement of a column and its load or entablature. There are technically five of these: Tuscan, Doric, Ionic, Corinthian and Composite. Prac-

ORDER. (Cont'd)

tically there are but three for the Tuscan is a clumsy Doric and the Composite is a fusion of the Corinthian and the angular Ionic. It would be hard to find Tuscan or Composite in Colonial work.

——TUSCAN. This has few distinguishing features.

——DORIC. Both mutular and denticular have triglyphs, *q. v.*, but our ancestors often omitted mutules and triglyphs.

——IONIC. The classic Ionic has a capital with volutes which are set parallel to the architrave above. The Scamozzi type, so-called, which is really of ancient origin, is the prevalent form in Colonial work. It has volutes turned outward at an angle of forty-five degrees. This was really an ancient form preferred because all four of its sides looked alike. With this order Palladio used a cushion frieze, *q. v.* Both Palladio and Scamozzi used modillions in the cornice though the classic form does not.

——CORINTHIAN. Here the capital has two rows of leaves and there are small volutes under the corners of the abacus which has curved sides in plan. The entablature is plain except for carving. There are modillions in the cornice.

——COMPOSITE. Here the Corinthian leaves are joined to the volutes of the angular Ionic. The cornice has no modillions.

OVERHANG. The projection

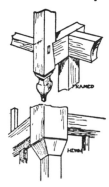

of one story beyond that below. *See* Jetty.

——FRAMED. With separate posts.

——HEWN. With continuous posts.

OVOLO. The quarter-round moulding. *See* Moulding.

PACE. A platform *See* Footpace, Half-pace, Quarter-pace.

PALLADIAN WINDOW. This name seems to be late. *See* Venetian window.

PANEL. In woodwork a board planed to a featheredge. Each of its four sides is set into a frame of stiles and rails, *q. v.*, or into a bolection mould-ing, *q. v.* The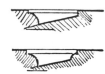

panel itself may be plain, or raised-and-bevelled, or raised-beaded-and-bevelled. It may also be plain with mouldings planted on its face.

PANEL BACK. A panel under a window sill, inside the house.

PANELLING. A series of panels: (*a*) over the whole room; (*b*) over the whole fireplace end; (*c*) around the room up to the windows or higher, or a combination of *b* and *c*. Panelled ceilings occur.

PANTRY (Fr. *pain*). The place where the bread and dry provisions were kept.

PARLOR. Originally a room in a monastery where conversation was allowed. The withdrawing room—"company room" of the house, across the entry from the hall.

PARLOR CHAMBER. The bedroom above the parlor.

PEDESTAL. A moulded block, with base, dado or die, and surbase, which was set beneath a column or pilaster. Usually seen in mantelpieces and outside doorways of the early eighteenth century.

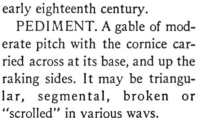

PEDIMENT. A gable of moderate pitch with the cornice carried across at its base, and up the raking sides. It may be triangular, segmental, broken or "scrolled" in various ways.

PIER. The mass of masonry at each side of an arch. A mass of masonry to support a large beam.

PILASTER. A flat, slightly projecting mass doing duty as a column and given all the details of the latter.

PIN. A round piece of hard wood used to fasten mortises and tenons together. In the panel work they were usually pine. In frames of oak they were somewhat roughly made to prevent turning in the joint. *See* Draw-Bore Tenon. Large pins were called treenails, *q. v.*

PITCH. The ratio of the rise of a roof to its span, as one third pitch. The rise in a given number of feet.

PLANCER (PLANCEER). (Fr. *plancher*.) The soffit of a cornice, *q. v.* "Plancer" can still be heard among carpenters.

PLASTER CORNICE. On the outside these are fairly early and take the form of a plastered cove. *See* Rafter, Knee. On the inside they appear with the Adams and Asher Benjamin.

PLATE. The beam framed on the tops of the posts to carry the common rafters and to tie the house lengthwise. *See* Frame, Summer.

POST. A heavy upright piece of timber set at each corner of the building, and at intervals between, to carry the girts and the plates and through them the floors and the roof. The posts are framed into the sills and the plates and the girts are framed into the posts. *See* Frame, Summer.

POST BRACKET. A projec-

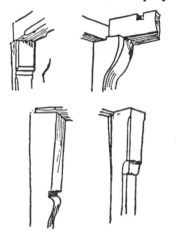

tion at the head of a post to enlarge the bearing space.

POST FLARE. A straight or

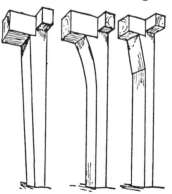

curved enlargement of a post, from the floor up, to do the work of the post brackets while saving a goodly amount of hewing.

PURLIN. A beam framed between the principal rafters on

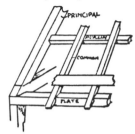

each side of a roof to carry the common rafters or simply vertical boarding.

——ROOF. A roof boarded vertically directly on purlins with no common rafters.

QUARREL. A lozenge-shaped piece of glass set in lead "cames," *q. v.*

QUARTER. *See* Stud.

QUARTER GRAIN. Wood sawed or riven parallel to the grain, "grainway" in modern parlance. Used mostly of oak, as quartered oak. *See* Wainscot.

QUARTER-PACE. The corner landing in a stair with three runs, *q. v. See* Pace.

QUEEN POST. A vertical post, one of a pair, in a truss over a wide span. It, like the King post, *q. v.*, is really a tie. *See* Truss.

QUIRK. A cutting back of the upper part of a moulding under

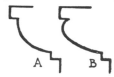

the fillet. This form, except in the bead, is characteristic of Asher Benjamin's time. It is shown at B in the cut, a quirked ovolo while A gives the regular form. *See also* Bead, Quirked.

QUOINS. Square stones set at the corners of a brick or stone

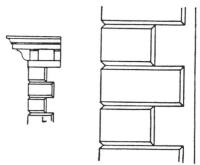

building. Imitation of these in woodwork.

RABBET (REBATE). A rectangular sinkage at the corner of a piece of framing or finish, generally to receive another piece joined thereto.

RAFTER (PRINCIPAL). The beam forming the slope of a roof truss, *q. v.*

——COMMON. One of the smaller beams which run over the purlins, *q. v.*, from plate to ridge and carry the roof boarding.

——KNEE OR BENT TREE PRINCIPAL. A principal rafter so cut

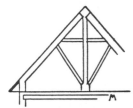

from a tree branch as to have at its foot a bend or "knee" which comes down on the plate at a right angle as is shown in the cut from Moxon (M). The object was to provide for a plastered cove cornice without an extra plate, as is shown in

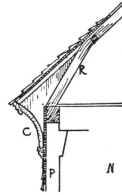

the sketch (N) from an actual example in Newport. This is perhaps the last descendant of the old English "Curved Tree Principal," shown by Mr. C. E. Innocent in his *Development of*

RAFTER. (Cont'd)

English Building Construction, ch. IV, figures 8 and 9.

RAIL. The horizonatal pieces carrying the panels in doors and other panelwork. The sloping or horizontal bar which guards the side of a stair well or other opening.

RAKE. A slope, as of a gable, or a stair string.

RAKING CORNICE. The cornice along the rake or slope of a gable or pediment. *See* Barge Board, Pediment.

RAMP. The upward turn of a stair rail to bring it to a mitre

with the level rail above. The opposite of an ease. Often called by workmen a "gooseneck."

READER'S DESK. The middle compartment of a "three-decker" pulpit, *q. v.*

REEDING. A series of convexities, like a bundle of reeds, the opposite of flutes, used in place of the latter in columns and pilasters and elsewhere.

RETURN. To carry a moulding around a corner against the surface from which it projects. Also used of the part of the moulding so treated.

RIDGE. The peak of a roof, the line of the tops of the rafter joints.

RIDGEPOLE. A small beam into which the tops of the rafters are framed. Very rare.

RIFT. Wood split or sawed with the grain. *See* Quarter Grain, Riven.

RISE. The height of a stair step from tread to tread.

RISER. The vertical board at the front of a step.

RIVEN. Split as in old clapboards, and some early plank. *See* Rift, Frow. *Cf.* the *geklofte eik* of the Plymouth fort.

RUBBED BRICK. Brick rubbed to give them a smoother surface and a lighter color. Common in Virginia.

RUBBLE. Field stone or roughly quarried stone, shaped with the hammer.

RUMFORD FIREPLACE. Invented by Count Rumford. Triangular in plan it throws more heat into the room than the common type, partly, perhaps, because the fire itself is brought further forward.

RUSTICATION. An emphasis of the joints in the stone work of walls by a square or V-shaped sinkage. The same treatment is also imitated in woodwork.

SASH (Shas. Fr. *chasser*). A wooden frame filled with leaded glass, or with glass set in wooden bars or muntins. There are two sash in a window and the lower sash is movable up and down. It differs from a casement in having this vertical motion while a casement swings out. It appears in England at Whitehall in 1685.

SASH WEIGHT. A mass of metal, probably lead, to counterweight the sash.

SAW PIT. A pit over which the log to be sawed was laid and in which the "pit man" stood at the lower end of the vertical "pit saw" while the "top sawyer" stood over the log above.

SCOTIA (OR HOLLOW). A moulding the reverse of the Torus, *q. v.*

SCROLL. A spiral turn at the end of a stair rail at the beginning of the lowest run.

SHEATHING. Boards one inch thick, or even less, generally of pine, soft or hard, but sometimes of whitewood or chestnut or even of oak. The boards are set vertically or horizontally—the latter is usual on the side and end walls of studded houses. The edges of the boards are moulded, or are feathered, for the joints

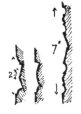

and narrow boards are inserted between the wide ones at intervals.

SHIPLAPPING. Shaving the ends of clapboards and bevelling

the edges of outside boarding to keep out water.

SHUTTER. A solid blind, used inside or outside. The early inside shutter slid in a groove or on a track on the window stool and its continuation, the chair rail. Later the shutter was hung double on each side as in England.

SHUTTER BOX. A space or pocket on each side of a window to receive the folded double-hung shutters.

SILL. The heavy timber on the foundation of a building. It carried the posts and studs of the walls, and the framing of the first floor as well. *See* Frame, Ground Sill. The bottom crosspiece of a window frame. *See* Stool Casing. A threshold.

SLITWORK. Sawing three-inch plank, or even one-inch boards lengthwise to reduce their thickness to one inch or even one half inch.

SOFFIT. The underside of a projection, as a cornice, or of an architrave. *See* Plancer. Also used of the intrados, *q. v.*, of a vault, *q. v.*

SPIRE. The staged and pointed portion of a steeple above the tower.

STACK OF CHIMNEYS. What we understand by chimney —the whole mass fireplace, flues, and outside stack. 1662.

STAFF BEAD. The moulding around a window or door frame in a brick wall, close to the brickwork, to stop water.

STAIR. A succession of steps leading from one floor to the next above or below.

——BLOCK STEP OR SOLID STEP. Two parallel sloping beams— the "pair of stayers" to which

are pinned sections of wood beams split or sawed on their diagonals. A few cellar stairs of this type have been found.

——SOLID NEWEL.

Dog-leg. In this type the strings, with the rail and balusters are over each other, so that there is only one post at the turn and thus no open well.

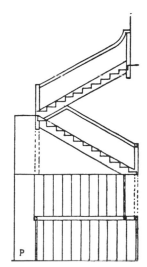

Zig-Zag. Box steps alternately on one side and the other between walls.

——OPEN NEWEL. Square or rectangular plan. *See* Scroll.

Circular or Oval Plan. These, except for the cir-

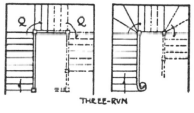

THREE-RUN

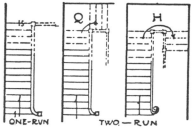

ONE-RUN   TWO — RUN

One-run.   Two-run.

Three-run.

cular stair in the Old State House in Boston, are really Post-Colonial.

Half circle joining two runs.

Continuous curve, all winders.

Right-hand.

Left-hand. With the rail of the balustrade on the right or left in ascending.

STAYER. *See* Stair, Block Step.

STEEPLE. The combination of tower and spire.

STEP. Originally a block of stone on a masonry foundation; or a short beam bevelled and fastened to two "stayers." *See* Stair, Block Step. Later steps were built up of a horizontal board for the tread and a vertical board for the riser.

STEP BRACKET. An ornament on the string at the end of a step, jig-sawed or carved, often very elaborately.

STILE. The vertical strip at the side of a panel and between two panels. *See* Rail.

STOOL CASING. The flat member with the moulding and "apron" below it on the inside of the sill of a window.

STRING. The support of the steps of a stair.

——OUTSIDE OR FRONT. May be a "closed" or "box" string which is of one width through-

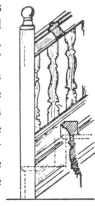

out and is moulded and shows no steps, or an "open" string which is cut out for the steps the ends of which are thus clearly defined. The former type is the older.

——WALL. The finished string against the wall.

STUD. The upright stick, roughly 3 x 4, which, in a stud house, fills the spaces between the sills, posts, girts and plate. It is an old English provincial word which came over with the settlers. The usual English word for what we still call a "stud" is "quarter."

SUMMER. The heavy beam which crosses the ceiling of a room from girt to girt and carries the joists of the floor above.

——LENGTHWISE. Parallel with the front wall of the house.

——THWARTWISE. Parallel with the end wall and thus at right angles with the front wall.

——DIAGONAL. *See* Dragon Beam.

——CROSSED. A lengthwise and thwartwise summer framed together in mid ceiling. Several examples exist.

(See illustrations on next page)

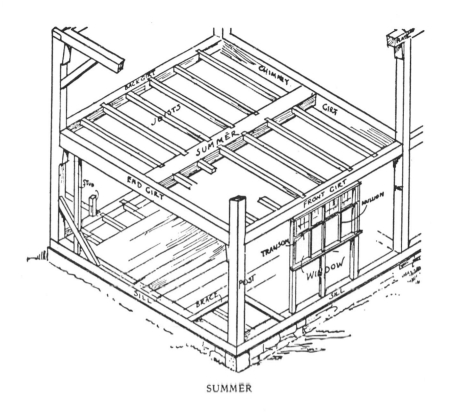

SUMMER

CROSSED SUMMER

SURBASE. The upper moulding of a Pedestal, *q. v.*, or of low panelling, or carried around without panels.

TENON. A short projection from the end of a beam. It is pinned into a mortise, *q. v.* See also Tusk.

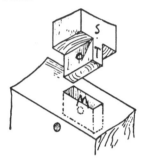

THATCH. Coarse grass used for roofing as in England.

THREE-DECKER. A common name for an early pulpit,

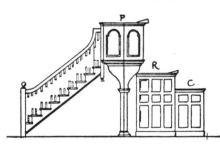

with its three parts, Pulpit, Reader's desk, *q. v.*, and "Clark's" desk.

TIE BEAM. A beam connecting the feet of the principal rafters of a truss to prevent them from spreading. In the ordinary houses the girts in the third floor act as ties.

TORUS. A moulding which is a half-round or a little more, in section. *See* Moulding.

TRANSOM. A piece of wood framed between or across the mullions of a window, or across an arched window or door. *See* Mullioned Window.

TREENAILS. Pins used in framing.

TRIGLYPH. A slightly projecting rectangular slab in the Doric frieze.

TRUSS.

RAFTERS AND TIE BEAM

RAFTER TIE AND COLLAR

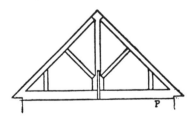

KING-POST TRUSS (P-Pain)

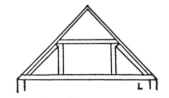

QUEEN-POST TRUSS (L-Langley)

TRUSS. (Cont'd)

Essentially a triangle formed by two rafters and a tie beam, *q. v.*, for the support of a roof with or without collar joist. To this may be added a king post, *q. v.*, or two queen posts, *q. v.*, and certain braces.

TUSK TENON. A sort of

tenon with one sloping shoulder used in early floor joist.

TUSK AND TENON. A tenon

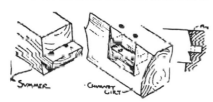

with a tusk below it, used in large beams.

TYPE. An old word, common in Wren's time and even much later, for the sounding board of a pulpit.

UNDERPINNING. The stone or brick wall which rose a foot or more above the ground to support a wooden building—where there was no cellar it was generally only "shovel deep." When there was a cellar it stood on the cellar wall and formed a continuation thereof.

VALLEY. The re-entrant angle formed by the meeting of two roof-slopes, the ridges of which

are at right angles. Two parallel roofs, the eaves whereof meet, also form a valley, at the bottom. Such construction was used in England and not unknown here.

VAULT. A ceiling arched in various ways.

——1. BARREL VAULT. A continuous arch for the length of the room.

——2. DOMICAL VAULT. A dome, generally quite flat.

——3. GROINED VAULT. Formed by the intersection of two cylinders.

VENETIAN DOOR. In England, a door with sidelights. *See* Window, Venetian.

VOUSSOIR. One of the wedge-shaped stones or one of the bricks of which the ring of an arch is built.

WAINSCOT. Originally this meant quartered oak. It was later transferred to the panelling made of it. Our ancestors used it to mean sheathing or ceiling (sealing). *See* Winthrop's rebuke to Ludlow in his Journal.

WATER TABLE. A slope, plain or moulded, at the top of the underpinning or at the first floor level or offset.

WEATHER BOARDING. Wide boards, bevelled on one edge, and lapped like clapboards.

WELL HOLE. The opening around which a stair run is built, an open newel. *See* Newel.

WIND BRACE. A brace from a principal rafter to a purlin.

WINDERS. Steps with radiating risers and thus narrowing treads. *See* Flyers.

——MULLIONED. Divided by mullions into two or more lights.

——CASEMENT. With glazed frames swinging out.

——TRANSOM. With a horizontal division, with or without mullions.

——SASH. (Fr. *chasse*). With sash sliding up and down.

——VENETIAN (*Vernition*). A group of three windows. The central one is wider and taller

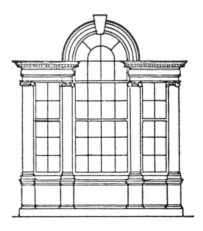

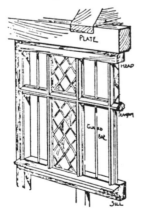

WINDOW.
——SINGLE. One opening.

than the rest and is round-headed. The two side windows are square-headed. *See* Palladian. Perhaps any window with sidelights and an elliptical toplight. *See* Venetian Door.

The Dating of Old Houses

by

DR. HENRY C. MERCER, OF DOYLESTOWN, PA.

T HE following observations are based upon notes taken upon the recent examination of about one hundred and twenty old houses in Bucks county and Philadelphia, Pennsylvania, built in the eighteenth and early nineteenth centuries, and it seems probable that the conclusions apply not only to old dwellings in Pennsylvania, but also to those in New York, New England, and the Southern states, where the same builders' material, carpenters' methods, tools and hardware were used during the period in question.

The conclusions are as follows: that old houses may be dated within reasonable limits by (1) the nails used; (2) the hinges; (3) the door panels; (4) the wrought-iron thumb-latches; (5) the Norfolk latches; (6) the cast-iron thumb-latches; (7) the wood-screws; and (8) the sawed laths.

WROUGHT NAILS.

Handmade (wrought) nails (Fig. 1), of soft malleable iron, with rectangular shanks, drawn by hammer blows to a point and

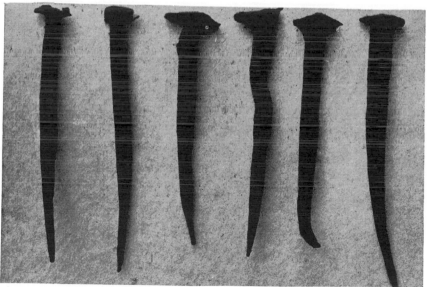

FIG. 1.—WROUGHT-IRON NAILS.

In general use until 1796-1798. From garret floors of old houses near Philadelphia. (A) Warner House, near Pineville, Pa., dated 1769. (B) "J. C." House, near Wormansville, Pa., dated 1784. (C) Brucker House, near Keelersville, Pa., before 1776. (D) Paxson-Hall House, near Doylestown, Pa., before 1776. (E) Graeme Park, near Horsham, Pa., dated 1721. (F) Brown ("I. B.") House, near Gardenville, Pa., dated 1765.

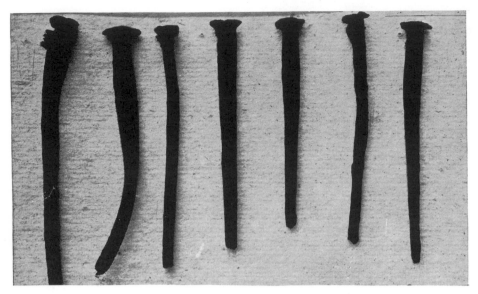

FIG. 2.—CUT NAILS—HAMMER-HEADED.

In general use from 1796-8 to *c.* 1827. Speciments removed from original garret floors of old houses in Bucks County, Pa. (A) Wenderbelt House, near Wormansville, *c.* 1800. (B) Ott Log House, Doylestown, *c.* 1806. (C) Bean's House, near Mechanicsville, dated 1804. (D) Reeds Mill, Castle Valley, dated 1815. (E) S. S. Myer's House, Pipersville, dated 1816. (F) S. Fluck House, near Deep Run, dated 1820. (G) Yoder House, near Silver-dale, dated 1820.

FIG. 3.—CUT-NAILS—STAMP HEADED.

In general use after *c.* 1825. Speciments removed from garret floors of old houses in Bucks County, Pa. (A) Grier House, near Dublin, dated 1827. (B) Sullivan Tenant House, near Keelersville, *c.* 1833. (C) Swartzlander-Gayman House, near Doylestown, dated 1838. (D) Bryan House (Stanley Rapp), near Fountainville, 1840. (E) Stear House, near Dublin, dated 1834. (F) L. Yoder's Desk, dated by pointed wood screws, after 1846.

with clearly hammer-marked heads, were from time immemorial, universally used in house building, until about 1800 (in Philadelphia, 1797) when cut nails (Fig. 2), because of their much greater cheapness, everywhere immediately superseded them. Therefore, where the original nails of a house are wrought (see Fig. 1), the house dates before about 1800; or, where cut, vice versa, after that date.[1]

All the evidence examined establishes this fact, with the following exceptions; namely, that long after 1800, wrought nails, to stand the jar, and because they would clench, continued to be used in the facings of window shutters; in the battens of doors; in the overlap of boards (old style) in lathed room partitions; or on door latches, etc., until about 1850. But these exceptions are not typical of the nails used to build houses after 1800. Nails used at the time a house was built are nearly always to be found in the garret floors.

The wrought nail (Fig. 1), no matter what its size, as generally used in house construction, is easily distinguished from the machine-made nails, called cut nails (Figs. 2 and 3), above referred to, and described later. It was made from rectangular strips of malleable iron, several feet long, and about a quarter of an inch thick, called nail rods, which were furnished to the blacksmith or nailer, who, holding one of them in one hand, heated its end in his forge, and then, on the anvil, pointed it with the hammer on

[1] Later evidence may show that cut nails came into general use in New England two or three years earlier than in Pennsylvania. Knight's *American Mechanical Dictionary* (cf. "Nail Making Machine") says that Jeremiah Wilkinson of Cumberland, Rhode Island, about 1775, cut tacks from plates of sheet metal and afterwards (date not given) made nails also; and that Ezekiel Reed of Burlington, Mass., invented a machine for cutting nails from the plate in 1786. J. L. Bishop's *History of American Manufactures* says that Jacob Perkins of Newburyport, Mass., invented in 1790, a machine for making cut nails and patented "a machine to cut and head nails at a single operation" in 1795. Bishop also speaks, without definite dates, of Thomas Odiorne and Jesse Reed as early cut-nail inventors. The Essex Institute, at Salem, Mass., exhibits a model of Nathan Read's machine for cutting and heading nails at a single operation patented by him on January 8, 1798.

Unfortunately, the very important records of the United States Patent Office, between 1791 and 1836, including the patents and drawings, have been destroyed by fire, leaving only a bare dated list of the issues, often lacking the locality of the patentee. They show cut-nail patents issued as follows:

FOR A NAIL-CUTTING MACHINE. Omitting localities of patentees:—J. Peerson, March 23, 1794; J. Perkins, January 16, 1795; A. Whittemore, November 19, 1796.

NAIL-HEADING MACHINE. J. Byington, December 23, 1796; J. Frost, December 23, 1796.

NAIL-HEADING AND CUTTING MACHINE. L. Garritson, November 16, 1796; G. Chandlee, December 12, 1796; J. Kersey, February 24, 1797; J. Nevill, August 12, 1797; J. Spence, February 16, 1797; N. Read, January 8, 1798.

Notwithstanding the fact that these patents were granted, the evidence of the nails themselves, and the notes quoted later, on N. Read's (1798) machine from Bentley's *Diary*, and from Whitaker's *Narrative*, show that the last two kinds of machines were not efficient until about 1817 to 1820.

all four sides. Next, he partly cut it, above the point, on the "hardy," with a hammer blow, and then, inserting the hot point into the swage hole, he broke off the rod and hammered the projecting end so as to spread it around the top of the hole; after which, the cooling, shrunken nail was easily knocked out of the orifice.

Wrought nails, as free-hand forged products (Fig. 1), vary greatly in style and shape, but the evidence examined has not as yet furnished any definite date for any of their variations.

CUT NAILS AFTER 1800.

The far more easily made cut nail (Figs. 2 & 3), as the evidence clearly shows, consists of a rectangular, tapering shank of iron, not hammered into a point by hand, but tapered, by a single cut, across a plate of iron. The smith was here furnished, not with a nail rod, but with a strip of plate iron, several feet long, about two and a quarter inches wide, and often about one-eighth of an inch thick. This strip he slid into a cutter, worked at first by hand-power, resembling those used by bookbinders to trim books, and not here shown. This cutter, rising and falling rapidly, clipped off the end of the iron plate crosswise into narrow, tapering, rectangular slices or nails, whose length was established by the width, and thickness, by the depth of the nail plate. The taper of the cut alone, produced the point, but not the head. This was made at first by dropping the freshly cut piece, point downward, into a slotted clamp or vise, and then spreading the larger projecting end with a hammer, as in the case of the wrought nail.

Cut nails are easily distinguishable from wrought nails by the following very apparent differences. Both have rectangular shanks, but the wrought nail (Fig. 1) tapers on all four sides; the cut nail (Figs. 2 and 3), on only two opposing sides; the latter nail being as thick (namely the thickness of the nail plate from which it was cut) at the point as at the head. Moreover, the two cut sides of the cut nail show very plainly, minute parallel striations, always absent on the wrought nail, marking the down smear of the cutter.

The evidence conclusively shows that these cut nails everywhere superseded the ancient wrought nail at the end of the eighteenth century, namely, not long after 1797, when two cut-nail factories had been established in Philadelphia, and, there-fore, if used by the builder, they will date a house as having been built after that year.

HAMMER HEADED CUT NAILS *c.* 1800 to *c.* 1825.

A still further examination of cut nails, from dated houses, shows that they may be distinguished into two classes; namely (*a*) those appearing between *c.* 1800 and *c.* 1825, with imperfect

FIG. 4.—CUT NAILS AFTER 1796.

(A) Rough sketch of cross-section of a cut nail, enlarged and exaggerated, showing down-smears of the cutter on opposite sides of the shank, proving that the nail-plate has been turned.

(B) Cross-section of a cut nail, enlarged, showing both down-smears of the cutter on the same side of the shank, proving that the nail-plate has not been turned.

or irregular heads, or, more particularly, hammered heads; that is, heads showing the facets of more than one hammer blow (Fig. 2), and (*b*) those appearing after *c.* 1825, and throughout the following century, with stamped heads, showing level tops impressed by a single blow or stamp (Fig. 3).

Information gathered with difficulty from the Patent Office records and books, makes it probable (subject to correction by dated nails) that in general, up to 1825, the nail-cutting machines had not been perfected; in other words, that while after 1825, nail machinery produced cut nails at a single operation, before that time, two machines, run by handpower, but not yet by steam, nor even by water, one to cut, as described above, and another, probably nothing more than a special vise to hold the shank while hand-hammering the head, were used in the manufacture of cut nails.

The hand-cranked machine, for cutting and heading nails at

one operation, patented by Nathan Read of Salem, Mass., in 1798 (See model at Essex Institute, Salem, Mass.), was not a success. Neither were any of the other "cutting and heading" machines, or simple "heading" machines, in existence or patented at that time, as is shown by the evidence of the nails themselves, and further. in the Diary of Rev. William Bentley, who visited Read's nail works in 1810 (See *Essex Institute Historical Collections,* April, 1918, page 113), and found that the workmen were then heading nails in the only way thus far successful, namely, by hand, "as it is found heading is done better by hand than by any machine as yet invented both as to time and goodness of execution."

Joseph Whitaker (See his manuscript diary in the library of the Bucks County Historical Society) was also thus making cut nails in Philadelphia, from 1809 to 1816-20, by a double operation; namely, cutting the plates with a hand-cranked machine and afterwards hammer-heading the shanks held in a clamp worked by a foot lever.

It further appears, that, at first, since the knife of the cutting machine was set diagonally so as to cross-cut the nail-plate into a tapered slice, the workmen had to turn the plate upside down at each stroke, so as to continue the taper by reversing the cut; and the very earliest cut nails (1800 to *c.* 1810) prove this fact by the down smear of the knife, round-edged above and sharp below, being reversed on the two opposing cut sides of the nail shank (See Fig. 4 A). They also show, that very early in the nineteenth century, this troublesome turning of the nail-plate was superseded by wriggling or staggering the blade of the cutter during the operation, so as to reverse the taper at each stroke without turning the nail-plate, as shown in the cross section of Fig. 4B.

At first, also, in order to dispense with the difficulty of the usual heading, angle-headed (L headed) and headless nails called "brads" (See Fig. 5), were made. But as these latter continued in use for certain purposes (often for floors) until long after the middle of the nineteenth century, their confused evidence should here be thrown out of consideration.

STAMP-HEADED NAILS AFTER *c.* 1825.

An examination, not only of the records above mentioned but also of dated nails, shows that about the year 1825, the cut-nail

FIG. 5.—CUT-NAILS, L HEADED AND HEADLESS.

Made at a single cut from the nail-plate. They appear in Pennsylvania immediately after 1796, and continue in use along with the more common early Hammer-Headed and later Stamp-Headed Cut-Nails. Sometimes found in floors, clapboards, etc. (A) Woodman House, near Wycombe, dated 1798. (B) Wenderbelt House, near Wormansville, c. 1820. (C) Werner House, near Gardenville, dated 1808. (D) Giants Grave House, c. 1820. (E) Grier House, near Dublin, dated 1827. (F) Sullivan Tenant House, near Keelersville, c. 1833.

FIG. 6.—WROUGHT-IRON DOOR HINGES, H AND HL TYPE, UNTIL 1776.

Specimens in Museum of the Bucks County Historical Society, Doylestown, Pa. (A) Wenderbelt House, near Wormansville. Inner door, old wing, c. 1770. (B-C) David Rittenhouse House, near Germantown, Pa.

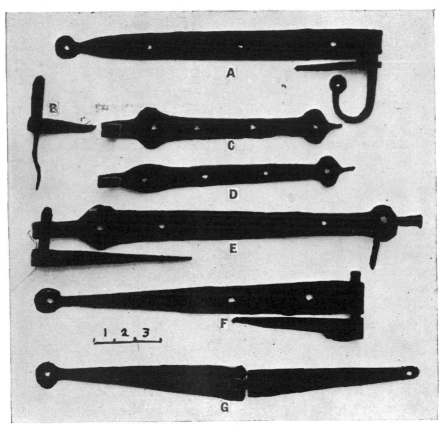

FIG. 7.—WROUGHT-IRON DOOR HINGES. "HOOK AND EYE' ALIAS
"STRAP" TYPE.

Used contemporaneously with H and HL wrought hinges on interior house
doors, until 1776, after which they continue in use on outer doors and shutters until c. 1850-60, and on barn doors until c. 1900. Specimens in Museum
of Bucks County Historical Society. (A) Brucker House near Kellersville,
showing spike hook with "rat-tail' before 1776. (B) Slifer Log House near
Keller's Church, spike hinge hook with untwisted "rat-tail,' c. 1750. (E)
Yost House west of Ottsville, showing plain spike hinge hook. (C. D. F. G.)
From the scrap-iron heaps of Bucks County junk dealers. (G) Wicket Hinge,
used on wickets opening in large barn doors.

machine, still working by water-power rather than by hand and not yet by steam, had been so perfected as to make cut nails no longer by two operations but by a single operation in one machine, in which the apparatus cut the nail, instantly clamped it and, at a single blow, stamped the head (See Fig. 3).

These stamped heads, at first (*c.* 1825 to 1830) comparatively thin, lopsided and imperfect, became more thick, square and typically regular after 1830 and are always easily recognizable after about 1840. But regardless of their variations, in any case, stamp-headed cut nails, if used in constructing a house, reasonably date it as after about 1825.

WROUGHT-IRON DOOR HINGES.

The evidence clearly shows that in the Colonial period in America, the common iron, house-door hinges were made always of wrought-iron until 1776 to 1783, when cast-iron hinges suddenly and universally took their place.

The old wrought hinges appear in two common varieties in the houses examined; namely, the so-called H or HL hinge, cut out of heavy sheet iron and fastened against the face of the door with screws or clenched wrought nails (See Fig. 6), or the "strap" or "hook and eye" hinge (See Fig. 7); namely, a long strap, bolted or nailed with clenched nails against the door and turning on a hook or gudgeon which latter was either spiked into the lintel,

Fig. 8.—CAST-IRON DOOR HINGES, BUTT HINGES.

After 1775 and until the present time. Cast-iron hinges were invented in 1775 (Izon and Whitehurst, British Patent, October 3, 1775). At end of American Revolution (1783) they immediately superseded the previously universal door hinge of wrought-iron. The specimen here shown in face and reverse is from a door in late wing of Wenderbelt House, near Wormansville, Bucks County, Pa., *c.* 1820.

or, where the lintel was too thin for spiking, set upon a plate, variously shaped, and sometimes strengthened with a projection or prop called a "rattail."

While the H and HL hinges (many of which were probably factory-made and imported from England) and nearly all of the strap-hinges, were found plain, a few of the latter, by no means typical and generally over-exhibited in museums, show floriated decorations.

It further appears that hand-made, wrought-strap hinges (still common in 1923 on barn doors in eastern Pennsylvania and elsewhere), continued to be used on outer house doors and window shutters, long after 1783, and hence, when so found, should be disregarded as proof of dates. But with these exceptions, the evidence abundantly shows, that where wrought hinges (generally HL, more rarely strap) are found on original *inner* house doors, they date the house as Colonial, or built before the Revolution.

CAST-IRON DOOR HINGES

Cast-iron door hinges, called butt hinges, comparatively small, compact, book-shaped, mortised into the edges, not set upon the faces of the door, of the common present type (See Fig. 8), because of their superior cheapness, came into universal use, no less suddenly, though a little earlier, than cut nails. They were invented in England by Izon & Whitehurst, and patented by British patent No. 1102, October 3, 1775, and were at first imported. After the interruption of British trade and house building by the Revolutionary War, they everywhere superseded the old wrought hinges, about 1784, after which they appear without significant exception, on all the dated houses examined by the writer. Hinges of this shape and name, i.e. butt hinges, of *wrought-iron* or brass, and never of cast-iron, had been made before 1775, generally for closets, or furniture, but none were found by the writer on room doors, in the houses examined. Cast-iron butt hinges also show differences and improvements in construction (not studied closely) after about 1800. But regardless of these variations and allowing for the above noted survival of wrought strap hinges on outer doors and shutters, these cast butt hinges,

FIG 9.—PLAIN CYCLO DOOR PANELS.

COLONIAL STYLE, MOULDING PLANED ON DOOR FRAME.

Casts from doors of old houses, dated between 1723 and c. 1776. Dates and names of houses of origin (in Bucks County and near Philadelphia, Pa.) marked on casts. (1682) Letitia Penn House. (1700) Old Swedes Church. (1721) Graeme Park. (1756) Neeleys Mills. (1765) Brown House. (1768) Buckingham Friends Meeting House. (1771) Woodman House. (1784) "— C." House.

FIG. 10.—QUIRKED OVOLO AND OGEE PANELS.

POST-COLONIAL STYLE, MOULDING PLANED SOLID ON DOOR FRAME.

Casts from doors of old houses, dated between c. 1776 and c. 1835. Dates and names of houses of origin (in Bucks County and near Philadelphia) marked on the casts. (1792) Neeley's Mills. Late wing. (1799) Radcliff House. (c. 1800) Horne House. Late wing. (1803) Horsham Friends Meeting. (1803) Swartzlander-Bergey House. (c. 1830) Sullivan Tenant House.

FIG. 11.—MACHINE-MADE DOOR PANELS, AFTER C. 1835.

Loose mouldings nailed on the frame to form the panels. Casts from original doors. (A) Dubois House, Court Street, Doylestown, dated 1833. (B) Swartzlander House, Sandy Ridge, dated 1838. Parlor door. (C) Chapman-James House, Doylestown, dated 1845. From bedroom door.

found upon the original doors of houses, will date the latter as post Colonial or built after *c.* 1776-1783.

QUIRKED, OVOLO DOOR PANELS, FROM *c.* 1776 TO *c.* 1835.

This examination of old houses has shown no more remarkable and unlooked-for fact than that the door panels, before *c.* 1776, if edged as usual with mouldings, always show a plain, i.e. unbeaded ovolo or quarter-round moulding on their outer margin (See Fig. 9), while immediately following the Revolution, after 1783, these same ovolo mouldings become scored with one or two quirks or beadings (See Fig. 10), or change into the ogee.

It seems probable that this observation will apply not only to door and shutter panels, but also to wall and furniture panels. Nevertheless, lacking sufficient information, as yet, we here limit it to doors where it is significant enough.

More probably caused by some technical change or improvement in joinery, not yet explained, than by mere fashion, this sudden, marked and universal change in door panels seems all the more surprising, since beaded or quirked ovolo and ogee mouldings appear elsewhere in the woodwork of old houses, as, for instance, in cornices and the framework of mantels. Further, since old carpenters' books describe hand-planes used to produce the latter mouldings considerably before 1776, it would seem reasonable to expect to find some exceptions to this rule; but the evidence of the houses in question shows none in the region examined, so that, subject to future correction, the information thus far gathered shows that hand-made door panels with plain ovolo frame work (See Fig. 9), if part of the original construction, will at once date a house as Colonial, or as built before *c.* 1776.

QUIRKED, OVOLLO DOOR PANELS. FROM *c.* 1776 TO *c.* 1835.

As above stated, the evidence gathered shows that after *c.* 1776, door or shutter panels, in which the outer frame consists of an ovolo moulding, with one or two beads or quirks (See Fig. 10), or an ogee, suddenly and universally supersede the old plain ovolo moulding, described as previously used, and continue in use on doors and shutters until machine-made mouldings take their place about 1835 (See Fig. 11).

In all the old houses examined, no significant exceptions to this rule, or survivals of old, plain ovolo panels, during the period in question, have been found, so that thus far, the evidence abundantly shows that the more ornate (i.e. beaded or quirked ovolo) door panels described, if part of the original construction of a house, will date it as built between *c.* 1776 and *c.* 1835.

MACHINE-MADE DOOR PANELS, AFTER *c.* 1835.

Besides the two significant changes in door panels, above noted, a third change, later but no less marked, took place in their construction upon the general introduction of wood-working machinery, wood-planing mills, etc., about 1835.

Revolutionary machines, of immense importance, to plane boards, make mouldings and otherwise work wood, had been invented in England by General Bentham, just before 1800 (See Knight's *American Mechanical Dictionary*) and no doubt were introduced into the United States and used about Boston, New York, Philadelphia, etc., between 1790 and 1835. Hence, very early machine-made door panels may be found later, in these and other old American cities, to prove the fact. But, in any case, these woodworking machines would have been run very restrictedly by water-power and not by steam, and the evidence shows that they were not established or their products used in the Pennsylvania country until after the general introduction of steam-power which gave birth to the modern factory about 1835.

Before that time, in the houses examined, all mouldings on door panels, whether of the plain or beaded ovolo or ogee type, above described, were hand-made and appear as solid parts of the panel, planed by hand-moulding planes upon its framework; while after that time they were machine-made and nailed on, as loose strips, around the sunken outer marginal recess of each panel (See Fig. 11).

It is not necessary for this purpose to consider the various sizes and shapes of these machine-made mouldings, nor to reason from the fact that they were introduced, not suddenly, but gradually, that the old styles of hand-made panels continued in use for a good while after their introduction. To discover that loose

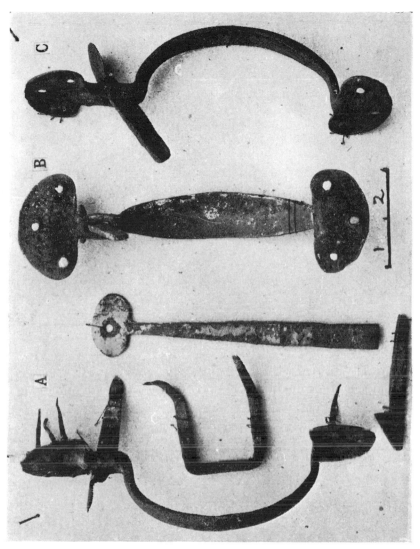

FIG. 12.—WROUGHT THUMB-LATCHES, BEAN-SHAPED AND
SWIVEL-LIFT, UNTIL C. 1840.

Commonest type of wrought thumb-latch. More and more frequent after *c.*
1750. Probably imported from England. Superseded by cast-iron, earthen
knob locks, etc., *c.* 1840. Cusp, shaped like a lima bean; Grasp flat; Lift,
always straight; Works on rivet perforating slot in grasp; Catch "Figure
Four" spike. (A) Showing wrought nails, bar and staple, from original door
in Wenderbelt House, near Wormansville, Bucks County, Pa. (old wing), *c.*
1770. Catch, contemporary type but not original with this latch. (B) From
original door in Bergey House, (old wing) near Doylestown, *c.* 1760-70. (C)
Bucks County Historical Society Museum, No. 15457. Not dated.

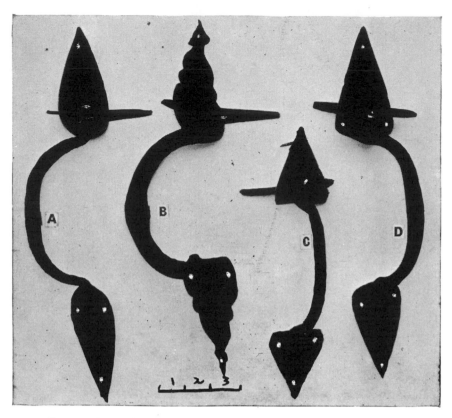

FIG. 13.—WROUGHT THUMB-LATCHES, PERFORATED CUSP TYPE,
UNTIL *C.* 1840.

Lift, generally straight, until *c.* 1800, works through hole in cusp with ad-
justable prong (as here shown but sometimes otherwise) to prevent its falling
out; Thumb press, flat; Cusps and Grasp more or less decorated. Large
elaborate forms used on outer doors. Curved lifts appear on these latches
after 1800-1825, and rarely before 1800. Sometimes these wrought latches
show swivel lifts (See Fig. 12). Specimens, not dated, in Museum of Bucks
County Historical Society, Doylestown, Pa. (A) Woodman House, near
Yycombe. (B) Chittick House, near Gardenville. (C) Horne House, near
Richlandtown, *c.* 1756. (D) Eastburn House, near Centre Hill.

strips of moulding have been nailed on around the sunken outer marginal recess of a panel is sufficient; that fact, where they are part of the original house construction, establishes the date of the house as not earlier than about 1835.

DOOR LATCHES WITH STRAIGHT LIFTS, BEFORE 1800.

Besides other door fastenings,—namely box knob locks, wooden latches, brass latches, German lever latches, boxed or unboxed, knob latches, etc., not here described, many original doors in old houses still standing, show their original wrought-iron thumb-latches, made of malleable iron by blacksmiths in five hammered pieces (Figs. 12 and 13), i.e. the hand grasp, an iron semi-circle; the lift, a lever with thumb press at one end penetrating the door to raise the bar; the bar thus lifted; the staple holding the bar against the door face; and the catch, a "figure 4" shaped, notched, iron piece, spiked into the lintel of the door, into which the bar falls.

These old latches are sometimes decorated (Fig. 13 B), but commonly plain (Fig. 13 A. C. D.), sometimes home-made (Fig. 13) and sometimes probably imported (Fig. 12). Sometimes they show their thumb-lifts fixed on swivels (the swivel-lift latch), (Fig. 12); sometimes they are notched into holes (the perforated cusp latch) (Fig. 13), and sometimes they appear with, but generally without, a knob or curl or pinch grasp on the bar. As yet no fixed types have been found to which dates may be ascribed beyond the following; namely, that the inner end of the lift, opposite the thumb-piece, commonly though not always appears straight before about 1800; after which it more and more often shows the familiar downcurve under the bar, characteristic of modern cast-iron latches. Doors latched with these straight-lift latches, some of which are very short, are sometimes hard to open, and sometimes, as if to remedy the difficulty, knobs or pulls appear on the bars of latches of early Colonial date. But these early knobed-bars are rare and it seems all the more remarkable that the very helpful down-curve above mentioned should not have been more generally used before 1800; nevertheless curved latch-lifts have been heard of by me, and seen by Mr. Frank K. Swain, in old houses in England, and in Pennsylvania, dating from the earlier period in question, e.g., several at the Community House,

Bethlehem, Pa., built about 1742, and several at the Letitia Penn House, Philadelphia, *c.* 1682 (doubtful).

Since the writing and first publication of this paper in *Old Time New England,* The Bulletin of the Society for the Preservation of New England Antiquities, for April, 1924, Mr. Albert H. Sonn has seen a curved lift-latch on a library door at Hadham, Conn., traced to an old mill built about 1740; one on a house at West Stockbridge, Mass., and one at Newfane, Vt., besides finding more recently a dozen or more in various parts of the eastern United States. Dr. A. Bertram Gilliland has also found several with scrolled, upturned lifts in the Stebbins House at Deerfield, Mass., built in 1772; one from the Pastor Williams House, Deerfield, built in 1770, and one at Washington's Headquarters, Newburg, N. Y., built before 1800. If more should appear later, the present evidence shows that they will continue to occur as exceptions, and that in general a curved latch-lift, if part of the original construction, will date a house after 1800.

THE NORFOLK LATCH, AFTER 1800.

The very conspicuous Norfolk latch (See Fig. 14), is easily distinguished from the wrought thumb-latches, in having its hand-grasp not enlarged at each end into plates, or cusps, but riveted upon a long, narrow, sheetiron escutcheon. Though long known in England as hand-wrought by local blacksmiths, it nevertheless appears in the American houses examined, as a *factory-made* and not smith-wrought product probably at first imported from England. Gradually taking the place about 1820 of the other forms of thumb-latch and competing with the knob-latch and the German lever latch (not shown here), it rivals, for a while, the newly invented earthen door-knob with cast-iron box, until it is generally superseded by the latter and by Blake's patent cast-iron thumb-latch of 1840 (Fig. 15).

The evidence shows that these factory Norfolk latches were made sometimes with, and sometimes without, a knob on the bar (Fig. 14); sometimes, at first, with a straight lift (A) and sometimes, later, with a curved lift (B and C), sometimes, at first, with a spiked catch (not shown here) and sometimes, later, with a catch perforating or riveted upon a plate (C). But without attempting to infer too much from these variations, we may at

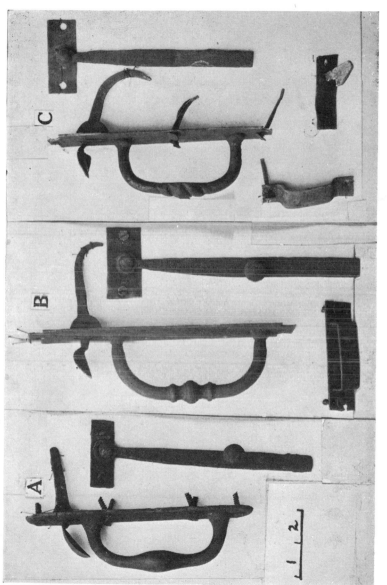

Fig. 14.—NORFOLK LATCHES, C. 1800 TO C. 1850.

Factory made, coming into general use soon after 1800. Finally superseded by cast-iron latches about 1850. Probably nearly all imported from England before c. 1835. Lifts, at first straight, gradually becoming curved after c. 1827, though straight lifts continue thereafter. (A) Ott Log House, Doylestown, c. 1809, spiked catch and staple missing; Saucer Press, straight lift, Knob on Bar Pointless Screws. (B) Grier House, near Dublin, dated 1827, Saucer Press, Curved Lift, Knob on Bar, Sheet Iron Staple, Catch missing, (C) Dennett House, Kittery, Maine. First half of 19th century. Curved Lift, Saucer Press, Sheet Iron Saple, Catch on Escutcheon.

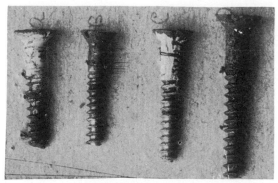

FIG. 17.—POINTLESS SCREWS, BEFORE 1846.

In universal use until 1846 when they were rapidly superseded by the pointed wood-screw. (Sloan's U. S. Patent, Aug. 20, 1846). (A) Octagon School House (Neeld), near Morrisville, Pa., c. 1820. (B) "J. C." House, near Wormansville in Bucks County, dated 1784. (C) Sullivan Tenant House, near Keelersville, Pa., c. 1833. (D) Fonthill Tenant House (from fire-place doors), Doylestown, Pa., c. 1842.

Henry Chapman Mercer.

Like Elbert Hubbard, Henry Ford, and Gustav Stickley, Mercer possessed a typical Arts & Crafts Period personality. In its purest form, it is a personality split with one half in the 19th century and the other in the 20th century. Mercer was an intensely individualistic person and, like Teddy Roosevelt's "Bully," the rhetoric of rugged individualism flows through his activities. Yet, he was a deeply religious man certain that art had no significance if it had no religious meaning. This belief sustained his first great Americana opus, *The Bible in Iron: Pictured Stoves and Stoveplates of the Pennsylvania Germans.* Mercer was an educated man, a lawyer, and a self-taught archaeologist who authored fifty-five scientific papers in a turgid career spanning 45 years.

Never able to afford a skilled retinue, the men he kept busy were a motley group unskilled workmen hired to construct his three pioneering concrete structures: "Fonthill" (1907-10), "The Moravian Tile Works" (1911-12), and "The Mercer Museum" (1913-16). "He's crazy," his workmen said. To most people, he lived an absurd life and died totally insane. Only today are we beginning to appreciate the work of this pioneer archaeologist, collector, museum creator, tile manufacturer & designer, scholar, author, and architect of concrete buildings.

Moravian: American Art Tile

least conclude, from the evidence, that the *factory-made* Norfolk latch, if contemporaneous with the building, will date a house between 1800 and 1840, or, allowing for survivals, 1850.

BLAKE'S CAST-IRON THUMB-LATCH, AFTER 1840.

Numerous dated examples found, show that Blake's typical cast-iron thumb-latch (Fig. 15), with circular catch-plate mortised and screwed into the door lintel, hollow patent bar-pivot, hollow staple guard, and saucer lift with opposite down-curve, patented by United States patent No. 1704, July 21, 1840, first came into general use on and after that year.

It seems probable that this latch was preceded by rare cast-iron experiments or improvements, i. e. cast-iron grasps on older wrought latches of the Fig. 12 type, etc., and was closely followed by evasive copies or patent infringements. But Blake's latch was, and still is, (1923) the cast-iron latch par excellence, and without concerning ourselves with earlier unpatented predecessors or variations of it or copies or patent infringements of its very typical

FIG. 15.—CAST-IRON THUMB-LATCH
AFTER 1840
Blake's U. S. Patent, No. 1704, July 21, 1840. First patented cast-iron door latch. Specimen shown set with its original pointless wood screws. From parlour door of Frayley-Trauger House, Pipersville, Bucks Co., Pa., built 1846.

catch or staple, this latch, when complete and original, as the evidence clearly shows, will date a house as built after 1840.

POINTLESS WOOD-SCREWS BEFORE 1846.

The unmistabable pointed wood screw, now universally used, was patented by United States patent No. 4704, August 20, 1846, before which time, all wood screws in general use, unless pointed by hand-filing, were blunt (Fig. 16).

Because these pointless screws would not start by driving into the wood, or penetrate, except by a previous gimlet hole, the pointed wood-screw suddenly and universally superseded them. Therefore, the wood-screw if pointless and original, will date a house before 1846; if pointed, after that date.

These facts, marking the end of the old house building period, though only applicable to the very latest buildings, are nevertheless important, since they may help to detect wholesale restorations or additions and show when kitchen fire-place doors stopped open-fire cooking, or where old latches, hinges, or doors have been shifted out of time or place.

SAWED LATHS, AFTER c. 1825 TO 1835.

Sawed laths (Fig. 17 A), i.e. thin strips of machine-sawed wood, about three feet long, by two inches wide, by a quarter of an inch thick, as keys for interior wall furring and partition plastering, first appear about 1825 to 1835. Though sawed, they were not produced by the water-run, vertical-frame saw of the old saw mills, but were first made by *circular saws,* about 1825 to 1835, on the general introduction of the circular saw, before which time, riven laths, i.e. hand-split with a frow and mallet, were invariably used (See Fig. 17 B), and no such thing as a sawed lath existed.

Riven laths were occasionally made and used for some time after the introduction of sawed laths, and therefore will not date a house as built before 1825, while sawed laths will, if original, date it as built after that time.

CONCLUSIONS.

In conclusion, it should be said in general, that in collecting and attempting to estimate the above facts, it soon became certain that very few of the old houses examined had escaped alterations

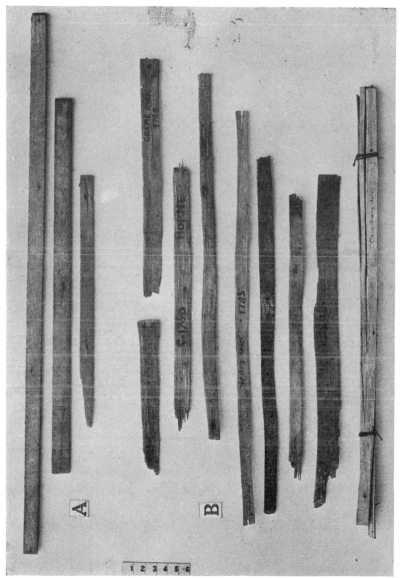

FIG. 16.—PLASTERING LATHS.

Hand split (riven) until about 1820 when the circular saw was introduced (Jackwith U. S. Patent, Mar. 16, 1820), and the mill-sawed lath (1820-1850) gradually came into use. (A) Mill-sawed lath, common type, later than 1820. (B) Riven laths from dated houses, 1722 to 1785. Those in bundle probably about 1840.

and repairs and therefore, unless the details above noted could be proved in each case to be part of the original construction, their evidence only led to error and confusion. With this reservation, reasonable certainty was always sought for and often found.

Very few houses appeared to have been raised or broadened. Therefore their original garret floors remained intact and the conclusive evidence of nails used therein, was easiest reached. When rarely, because of new floors, or L headed cut nails, this failed, we generally found it on staircases, in wash-boards or elsewhere in the house, and when, at times, this evidence seemed contradictory, some further fact, family tradition or historical record, showed that old doors or hinges, screws, or latches, had been inserted out of date into new houses, or vice versa.

Doors appeared original if set in original partitions; if frequently duplicated; if not cut down on their margins; and if with their hinges not covering old mortise nail or screw holes or outlines of removed hinges. Door panels; if on original doors; if frequently repeated or matching shutter panels. Latches; if often duplicated, and not betrayed as resettings by the marks of nail, screw or lift holes, etc., or of other door fastenings. Pointed or pointless wood screws; by their general use or appearance with otherwise original wood or iron work; and sawed laths; by their original use in partitions or in original furrings over rough unplastered walls.

Out of at least one hundred and fifty houses examined, about fifty were found dated by documentary evidence, or by date-plates or wall-stones; and the evidence of nails, woodwork and hardware, first studied in these dated buildings, always repeated and never contradicted itself in the undated houses examined later. As far as this evidence goes, it is very positive; but as yet, though quite definite after the Revolution, it fails to fix any subdivisions of time for the Colonial period (1650 to 1776).

QUEST OF THE COLONIAL
A BIBLIOGRAPHY OF BOOKS
1880 - 1930

IONIC

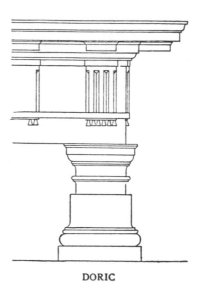

DORIC

CORINTHIAN

QUEST OF THE COLONIAL
A BIBLIOGRAPHY OF BOOKS
1880 - 1930

This bibliography of books on the American Colonial and Classical (Federal & Greek) Revivals published from the 1880's to 1930 began with the notion that the subject was languishing and about to fade (at last) into history. We were prepared to treat it as a historical curiosity, an amusing episode in the history of American taste. We intended neither to dismiss it nor revere it, but rather to show what books were responsible for its popularity. However, the Colonial & Classical Revivals have not faded and a recent holiday spent in the Middle West convinces us that it is still healthy. "Pilgrim," 17th century house types, with over-hangs, drop-finials, diamond-paned windows, and moldy green clapboards, dot the Middle West and are popular in such places as Cleveland, Toledo, and East Lansing (The Director of a Michigan Art Gallery calls these reproductions "Mid-West Gothic.") Meanwhile, the Middle West destroys their indigenous Victorian architecture with vengeance.

Interest in Colonial Architecture, Painting, Prints, and Decorative Art can be traced back to the middle of the (19th) century. Not until the 1880's though, did this become transformed into enthusiasm. At first, books were merely local catalogues of buildings, pictures, and objects. Then biographies began to appear. Finally, attempts at history were made. Against this pattern was imposed a constant, throbing romanticism supplied by such people as Alice Morse Earle, Anne Holingsworth Wharton, and Wallace Nutting. These and others (listed in the following bibliography) drove the Colonial Revival to fever pitch. During the '20's Wallace Nutting photos and his "States Beautiful" books adorned the parlors and bedrooms of gimcrack "Colonial" development houses. Auction prices for authentic antiques went higher and higher and peaked with the Reifsnyder Sale of 1929. Wallace Nutting supplied the upper Middle Class with his reproductions while Grand Rapids supplied other people with shoddy plywood imitations of the same thing (cf. *Furniture As Interpreted by the Century Furniture Company,* Grand Rapids, 1926).

The books were not alone responsible for the enthusiasm; the mass-circulation magazines must also be indicted. *Ladies Home Journal,* although it began the 20th century supporting such moderns as Frank Lloyd Wright, entered the '20's on the Colonial Bandwagon. *Saturday Evening Post, House Beautiful, Town & Country* and others led the parade. Newspapers were also involved. Charles Messer Stow rose to fame with a weekly column in the Friday edition of the now defunct New York *Sun.* The early '20's also saw the beginning (1922) of the successful *Antiques Magazine.* Then there were the museums. The opening of the American Wing of the Metropolitan Museum of Art in N. Y. C. (1924) sparked more interest in the Colonial than any other museum except Colonial Williamsburg, started in the '30's. Inspired by the American Wing, Henry Francis duPont began to collect American antiques and hired a former director of it (Joseph Downs) to administrate what ultimately became the Winterthur Museum. Prior to these museums, the Society for the Preservation of New England Antiquites had created a great deal of interest in the Colonial on its own. It inspired Henry Chapman Mercer to form at Doylestown, Pennsylvania, his collections of tools used by Colonists. This museum, completed in 1916, inspired Henry Ford to build one on the same model. All of the agencies — books, museums, magazines, auctions, reproductions, and newspapers — were the visible forces. Behind every thing were the antique dealers — dealers like the Sacks (now in a 3rd generation), Kindig, Walton, Ginsburg & Levy, etc. They found the antiques, studied them, became their connoisseurs and authenticated them.

Moreover, they created the collectors and their collections. From these collections museums, the American Wing, etc., were formed .

This bibliography ends at 1930 because books at that point began to be scholarly and critical. The romantic type of book, laced with pretty pictures of "Georgian" Colonial Architecture and interiors inhabited by costumed people existing in a never-never land went out of fashion. To be sure, during the '20's there were men like Fishe Kimball who did study Colonial Architecture as scholars. But most of the breed never rose to Kimball's calibre. More often they ranked with Harold Donaldson Eberlein.

Impatiently we still await the demise of the Colonial and Classical (Federal & Greek) Revivals. Perhaps it will never die. Then, in a hundred years, this country will be a land plastered with "Colonial" houses and "Colonial" furnishing — real, reproduction, and imaginary. All the Victorian buildings will have been destroyed and replaced with modern boxes, imitation Colonial rectangles, and split levels. Off in a corner perhaps there will be a heap of Victorian buildings & furnishings saved for the amusement of Americans who hide their shame of the non-Colonial with laughter. While on the subject of laughter, some people in the '20's (believe it or not) were ready to laugh at the Colonial and the collecting of Colonial Antiquities. Although a bit dated, *The Collector's What-not* (Boston, 1923) contains a lot of amusement for those prepared for it.   ·

Two other bibliographies we recommend are Henry Russell Hitchcock's *American Architectural Books* (1962) and John Freeman's *Prints Pertaining to America* (1963). The majority of the following books are from the Yorker Yankee Village Libraries at Old Irelandville.

Allen, Charles Dexter. *American Book-Plates* (1905).
American Children's Books Printed Before 1800, Exhibition of (1928).
Andrews, William Loring. *An Essay on the Portraiture of the American Revolutionary War . . .* (1896).
..... *An Index to the Ilustrations in Valentine's Manuals* (1906).
Fragments of American History Illustrated Soley by the Works of Those of Our Own Engravers Who Flourished in the XVIIIth Century (1898).
Atwater, Mary Meigs. *American Hand-Weaving, Its History* (1928).
Bacon, Leonard. *The Genesis of New England Churches* (1874).
Barker, Edwin Atlee. (1851 - 1916). Director of the Pennsylvania Museum and School of Industrial Art, 1907 - 1916.
..... *American Glassware, Old and New* (1900).
..... *Anglo-American Pottery; Old English China with American Views* (1899). Another edition in 1901.
..... *The Ceramic Collector's Glossary* (1914).
..... *Lead-Glazed Pottery: Plain Glazed, Sgraffito and Slip Decorated Wares* (1907).
..... *Marks of American Potters* (1904).
..... *Pottery: Catalogue of American Potteries and Porcelains* (1893).
..... *The Pottery and Porcelain of the United States* (1893). Other editions in 1901, 1909.
..... *Salt Glazed Stoneware, Germany, Flanders, England and the United States* (1906). Another edition in 1907.
..... *Tin Enameled Pottery* (1906). Another edition in 1907.
..... *Tulip Ware of the Pennsylvania-German Potters, An Historical Sketch of the Art of Slip-Decoration in the United States* (1903).
Bates, Albert C. *An Early Connecticut Engraver and His Work* (1906).
Bolton, Charles Knowles. *Bolton's American Armory* (1927).
Brock, Henry Irving. *Colonial Churches in Virginia* (1930).
Bulfinch, Ellen Susan (ed.). *The Life and Letters of Charles Bulfinch, Architect* (1896).
Camehl, Ada Walker. *The Blue-China Book: Early American Scenes and History Pictured in the Pottery of the Time* (1916).
Chamberlain, Nathan Henry. *A Paper on New England Architecture* (1858). Hitchcock calls this "probably the first separate publication on colonial architecture."
Chandler, Joseph Everett. *The Colonial Architecture of Maryland, Pennsylvania and Virginia* (1892). Another edition in 1900.
..... *The Colonial House* (1916). Another edition in 1924.

China Hunters Club, The, by The Youngest Member (1878).

Coffin, Lewis A. Brick Architecture of the Colonial Period in Maryland and Virginia (1919).

Corner, James M. and Eric Ellis Soderholtz. Architecture in New England (1891). Hitchcock calls this "the first photographic documentation of colonial architecture in book form."

Cousins, Frank and Phil M. Riley. Colonial Architecture (1912).

..... The Colonial Architecture of Philadelphia (1920). 975 copies printed.

..... The Colonial Architecture of Salem (1919). 1200 copies printed.

..... The Wood-Carver of Salem, Samuel McIntire, His Life and Work (1916). 930 copies printed.

Cunningham, Harry Francis. Measured Drawings of Georgian Architecture in the District of Columbia, 1750 - 1820 (1914).

Curtis, Mrs. Elizabeth (Gibbon). Gateways and Doorways of Charlestown, South Carolina (1926).

Denmark, E. R. Architecture of the Old South (1926).

Dexter, Henry Martin. Meeting Houses Considered Historically and Suggestively (1859).

Disosway, Gabriel Poillon. The Earliest Churches of New York and Its Vicinity (1865).

Drake, Samuel Adams. Old Boston Taverns and Tavern Clubs. (1917).

..... Our Colonial Homes (1894).

Dreppard, Carl W. Early American Prints (1930).

Dunlap, William. A History of the Rise and Progress of the Arts of Design in the United States (1834). Also published in a 3-volume 1918 edition.

Dyer, Walter A. American Furniture of the 18th Century (1934).

..... Creators of Decorative Styles (1917).

..... Early American Craftsmen (1915).

..... Handbook of Furniture Styles (1918).

..... The Lure of the Antique (1910).

..... The Rocking Chair: An American Institution (1928).

..... Sons of Liberty: A Story of the Life and Times of Paul Revere (1920).

Earle, Mrs. Alice (Morse) (1853 - 1911). Child Life in Colonial Days (1899).

..... China Collecting in America (1892). Another edition in 1924.

..... Colonial Dames and Good Wives (1895). Another edition in 1924.

..... Colonial Days in Old New York (1896).

..... Costume of Colonial Times (1894).

..... Curious Punishments of Bygone Days (1896).

..... Customs and Fashions in Old New England (1893). Another edition in 1894.

..... Home Life in Colonial Days (1898). Other editions in 1899, 1913.

..... In Old Narragansett: Romances and Realities (1898).

..... Margaret Winthrop (1895).

..... Old Time Gardens (1901). Published in two editions: one a 350 copy large paper edition. Another edition in 1916.

..... The Sabbath in Puritan New England (1891).

..... The Stadt Huys of New Amsterdam (1896). Another edition in 1896.

..... Stage-Coach and Tavern Days (1900). Another Edition in 1935.

..... Sun Dials and Roses of Yesterday (1902).

..... Two Centuries of Costume in America (1903).

Earle, Swepston (ed.) Maryland's Colonial Eastern Shore (1916).

Early American Trade Cards from the Collection of Bella C. Landauer (1927).

Eberlein, Harold Donaldson (d. 1964). The American Home Book of Decoration: Downstairs (1931) Upstairs (1931).

..... The Architecture of Colonial America (1915).

..... The Colonial Homes of Philadelphia and Its Neighborhood (1912).

..... Colonial Interiors, Federal and Greek Revival (1938).

..... Historic Houses of the Hudson Valley (1942).

..... Manor Houses and Historic Homes of Long Island and Staten Island (1928).

..... The Manors and Historic Homes of the Hudson Valley (1924).

..... Portrait of A Colonial City, Philadelphia, 1670 - 1838 (1939).

..... The Practical Book of Early American Arts and Crafts (1916). Other editions in 1927, 1936.

..... The Practical Book of Period Furniture (1914). Over 20 subsequent printings.

..... Practical Book of Interior Decoration (1919). Another edition in 1937.

Eggers, Otto R. Sketches of Early American Architecture (1922).

Elwell, Newton W. *Colonial Furniture and Interiors* (1896).

..... (comp). *The Architecture, Furniture and Interiors of Maryland and Virginia During the Eighteenth Century* (1897).

Embury, Aymar. *Early American Churches* (1914)

..... *The Dutch Colonial House* (1913). Other editions in 1919, 1929.

Faris, John T. *Historic Shrines of America* (1918).

..... *Old Churches and Meeting Houses In and Around Philadelphia,* (1926).

Foote, Henry Wilder. *Annals of Kings Chapel.* 3 vols. (1882 - 96).

Ford, Paul Leicester. *Check-List of American Magazines Printed in the Eighteenth Century* (1889).

Frederick R. Halsey Collection of Prints, The. 13 pts. (1916 - 1919).

Freese, John Wesley. *Historic Houses and Spots in Cambridge, Massachusetts and Nearby Towns* (1898).

French, Leigh. *Colonial Interiors, Colonial and Early Federal Periods* (1923).

Glenn, T. A. *Some Colonial Mansions and Those Who Lived In Them* (1898 - 1899).

Goforth, William Davenport. *Old Colonial Architectural Details In and Around Philadelphia* (ca. 1890).

Hale, Albert. *Old Newburyport Houses* (1912).

Halsey, R. T. H. and Charles O. Cornelius. *A Handbook of the American Wing* (1924).

..... and Elizabeth Tower. *The Homes of Our Ancestors* (1925).

Halsey, Rosalie V. *Forgotten Books of the American Nursery: A History of the Development of the American Story-Book* (1911).

Hammond, John Martin. *Colonial Mansions of Maryland and Delaware* (1914).

Hampton L. Carson Collection of Engraved Portraits, The 4 pts. (1904).

Harland, Marion (pseud. of Mrs. Mary Virginia (Hawes) Terhune). *More Colonial Homesteads and Their Stories* (1899).

..... *Some Colonial Homesteads and Their Stories* (1897).

Hart, Charles A. *Catalogue of the Engraved Portraits of Washington* (1904).

..... *Catalogue of the Works of American Artists in the Collection of Herbert L. Pratt* (1917).

Hayward, Arthur. *Colonial Lighting* (1923). Another edition in 1927.

Henkels, S. V. (comp.). *Rare Engraved Portraits of General George Washington and Other Notable Americans* (1906).

Historic Churches of America, Their Romance and Their History (ca. 1890).

Holloway, Edward Stratton. *American Furniture and Decoration, Colonial and Federal* (1928). Another edition in 1937.

Howe, Lois L. *Details from Old New England Houses* (1913).

Hufeland, Otto. *Historical Index to "Valentine's Manuals," 1841 - 1870* (1900).

Hunter, Frederick William. *Stiegel Glass* (1914).

Isham, Norman Morrison. *Early American Houses (1928).* 175 copies printed.

..... *Early Connecticut Houses* (1900).

..... *Early Rhode Island Houses* (1895).

Jackson, Joseph. *American Colonial Architecture . . .* (1924).

..... *Development of American Architecture, 1783 - 1830* (1926).

Kelly, J. F. *Early Connecticut Architecture.* 2 vols. (1924 - 1931).

..... *The Early Domestic Architecture of Connecticut* (1924).

Kettell, Russell Haves. *The Pine Furniture of Early New England* (1929). 999 copies printed.

Kimball, Fiske. *Thomas Jefferson, Architect* (1916).

..... *Domestic Architecture of the American Colonies and of the Early Republic* (1922).

Kingman, Ralph Clarke. *New England Georgian Architecture* (1913).

Knittle, Rhea Mansfield. *Early American Glass* (1927). Another edition in 1929.

Lathrop, Elise L. *Historic Houses of Early America* (1927).

Latrobe, Benjamin Henry. *The Journal of Latrobe* (1905).

Leiding, Harriette Kershaw. *Historic Houses of South Carolina* (1921).

Little, Arthur. *Early New England Interiors* (1878).

McClelland, Nancy. *Historic Wall-Papers . . .* (1924).

Major, Howard. *The Domestic Architecture of the Early American Republic — The Greek Revival* (1926).

(Metropolitan Museum, New York). *Measured Drawings of Woodwork Displayed in the American Wing* (1925).

Miller, Donald. *Measured Drawings of Some Colonial and Georgian Houses.*

3 vols. (1916 - ca. 1930).

Mills, Weymer Jay. *Historic Houses of New Jersey* (1902).

Moore, *Mrs.* Hannah Woodbridge (Hudson) (1857 - 1927).

..... *The Collector's Manual (1906).* Another edition in 1935.

..... *Delftware, Dutch and English* (1908).

..... *The Lace Book* (1904). Another edition in 1937.

..... *The Old China Book* (1903). Another edition in 1935.

..... *The Old Clock Book* (1911). Another edition in 1936.

..... *The Old Furniture Book, With a Sketch of Past Days and Ways* (1903). Another edition in 1936.

..... *Old Glass, European and American* (1924). Another edition in 1936.

..... *Old Pewter, Brass Copper, and Sheffield Plate* (1905). Another edition in 1933.

..... *Wedgewood and His Imitators* (1909).

Nason, *Mrs.* Emma (Huntington). *Old Colonial Houses in Maine Built Prior to 1776* (1908).

Northend, Mary Harrod. *American Glass* (1926). Another edition in 1936.

..... *Colonial Homes and Their Furnishings* (1912).

..... *Historic Doorways of Old Salem* (1926)

..... *Historic Homes of New England* (1914).

..... *Memories of Old Salem* (1917).

..... *We Visit Old Inns* (1925).

Nutting, Wallace (1861 - 1941). This Congregational Minister was advised by his physician to give up his ministry. He "retired" to his home in New England and mastered the art of photography as well as invented a process for coloring photographs. He made a small fortune from his "pallid prints of New England houses, gardens and woman in colonial costumes" that decorated Colonial Revival parlors & bedrooms from 1915 - 1930. Conquering semi-invalidism & deafness Nutting went on to write the following "States Beautiful" series illustrated, of course, with his photographs. He also was an authority on Early American furniture and satisfied the demand for the stuff by running a shop specializing in reproductions. Several of his craftsmen are still alive. Nutting also collected the real thing and sold his collection via J. P. Morgan to the Wadsworth Athenaeum in Hartford, Connecticut. Perusal of this bibliography reveals other practioneers of the art of romanticizing the Colonial Past (Earle, Wharton, etc.). Nutting was the master, the best known — they were second rate in comparison.

..... *The Clock Book* (1924). Another edition in 1935.

..... *Connecticut Beautiful* (1923) Another edition in 1935.

..... *Early American Ironwork* (1919).

..... *Furniture of the Pilgrim Century, 1620 - 1720, Including Colonial Utensils and Hardware* (1921). New edition in 1924.

..... *Furniture Treasury (mostly of American Origin) . . . 3 vols. (1928 - 1933).*

..... *General Catalogue* (1930 - ????).

..... *Maine Beautiful* (1924). Another edition in 1935.

..... *Massachusetts Beautiful* (1923). Another edition in 1935.

..... *New Hampshire* (1923). Another edition in 1937.

..... *New York Beautiful* (1927). Another edition in 1936.

..... *Old New England Pictures* (1913).

..... *Pennsylvania Beautiful* (1935).

..... *Pennsylvania Beautiful (Eastern)* (1924).

..... *Photographic Art Secrets, With a General Discussion of Processes* (1927).

..... *Vermont Beautiful* (1922). Another edition in 1936.

..... *Virginia Beautiful* (1930). Another edition in 1935.

..... *Wallace Nutting's Biography* (1936).

..... *Wallace Nutting Pictures, Expansible Catalog* (1915 -   ).

..... *A Windsor Handbook . . .* (1917).

Pelletreau, William Smith. *Early New York Houses* (1900).

Place, Charles Alpheus. *Charles Bulfinch, Architect and Citizen* (1925).

Robie, Virginia Huntington. *By-Paths in Collecting . . .* (1912).

..... *Historic Styles in Furniture* (1905).

..... *The Quest of the Quaint* (1916). Another edition in 1927.

Robinson, Albert Gardner. *Old New England Doorways* (1919).

St. Memin Collection of Portraits, The (1862).

Sale, *Mrs.* Edith Dabney (Tunis). *Boxwood and Terraced Gardens of Virginia* (1925).

..... *Colonial Interiors* (1930).
..... *Interiors of Virginia Houses of Colonial Times* (1927).
..... *Manors of Virginia in Colonial Times* (1909).
..... *Old Time Belles and Cavaliers* (1912).
Schuyler, Montgomery. *American Architecture* (1892).
Scott, Owen F. *Colonial Doorways: New York State* (ca. 1920's).
Shackleton, Robert (1860 - 1923) *The Book of Antiques* (1938).
..... *The Charm of the Antique* (1914).
..... *The Quest of the Colonial* (1913).
Shelton, William Henry. *The Jumel Mansion* (1916).
Shinn, George Wolfe. *Church Architecture* (1882).
Simms, Joseph Patterson. *Old Philadelphia Colonial Details* (1914).
Singleton, Esther (d. 1930). Author, editor, art and music critic. Author of 52 books. For seven years she was editor of *The Antiquarian*.
..... *The Collecting of Antiques* (1926). Another edition in 1937.
..... *A Daughter of the Revolution* (1915).
..... *Dutch New York* (1904).
..... *The Furniture of Our Forefathers.* 2 vols. (1901). Single volume editions in 1908, 1913, 1919.
..... *Historic Buildings of America as Seen and Described by Famous Writers* (1906).
..... *Historic Landmarks of America as Seen and Described by Famous Writers* (1907).
..... *Social New York Under the Georges, 1714 - 1776; Houses, Streets, and Country Houses, With Chapters on Fashions, Furniture, China, Plate and Manners* (1902).
..... *The Story of the White House* (1907).
Smith, Ralph Clifton. *A Biographical Index of American Artists* (1930).
Soderholtz, Eric Ellis. *Examples of Colonial Architecture in Charlestown, S. C. and Savannah, Ga.* (1895).
Spargo, John. *Early American Pottery and China* (1926).
Stauffer, David M. *American Engravers Upon Copper and Steel.* 2 vols. (1907)
Stokes, I. N. Phelps. *One Hundred Notable American Engravers, 1683 - 1850: Annotated List of Prints* (1925).
..... *The Iconography of Manhattan Island, 1498 - 1909.* 6 vols. (1915 - 1928).
Walbridge, William Spooner. *American Bottles, Old and New* (1920).
Wallington, Nellie Urner. *Historic Churches of America* (1907).
Wallis, Frank Edwin. *Old Colonial Architecture and Furniture* (1887).
..... *American Architecture, Decoration, and Furniture of the Eighteenth Century* (1896).
Ware, William Rotch. *The Georgian Period.* 3 vols. (1923). Compilation of a magazine series done in the 1890's.
..... *Seats of the Colonists and Other Furnishings* (1904).
Watkins, Lura Woodside. *Cambridge Glass (1818 - 1888) The Story of the New England Glass Company* (1930).
..... *The Development of American Glassmaking* (1935).
Westcott, Thompson. *The Historic Mansions and Buildings of Philadelphia* (1877).
Wharton, Anne Hollingsworth (1845 - 1928). *Colonial Days and Dames* (1895). Published in two editions: one in a 508 copy deluxe format.
..... *Heirlooms in Miniatures* (1898).
..... *In Old Pennsylvania Towns* (1920).
..... *A Last Century Maid* (1896).
..... *Martha Washington* (1897).
..... *Salons Colonial and Republican* (1900).
..... *Social Life in the Early Republic* (1902).
..... *Through Colonial Doorways* (1893). Published in two editions: one in a 442 copy deluxe format.
Whitefield, Edwin. *The Homes of Our Forefathers: Massachusetts* (1879), *Rhode Island and Connecticut* (1882), *Maine, New Hampshire and Vermont* (1886), *Boston, Old England and Boston, New England* (1889).
White Pine Series of Architecture Monographs, The. 22 vols. (1915 - 1936).
Wight, Charles Albert. *Some Old Time Meeting Houses of the Connecticut Valley* (1911).
Williams, Lenore Wheeler. *Sandwich Glass* (1922).
Wilson, Rufus Rockwell. *Historic Long Island* (1902).
..... *New England in Letters* (1904).
..... *New York: Old and New: Its Story, Streets and Landmarks* (1902).
..... *Rambles in Colonial Byways* (1901).
Wise, Herbert C. *Colonial Architecture for Those About to Build* (1913).